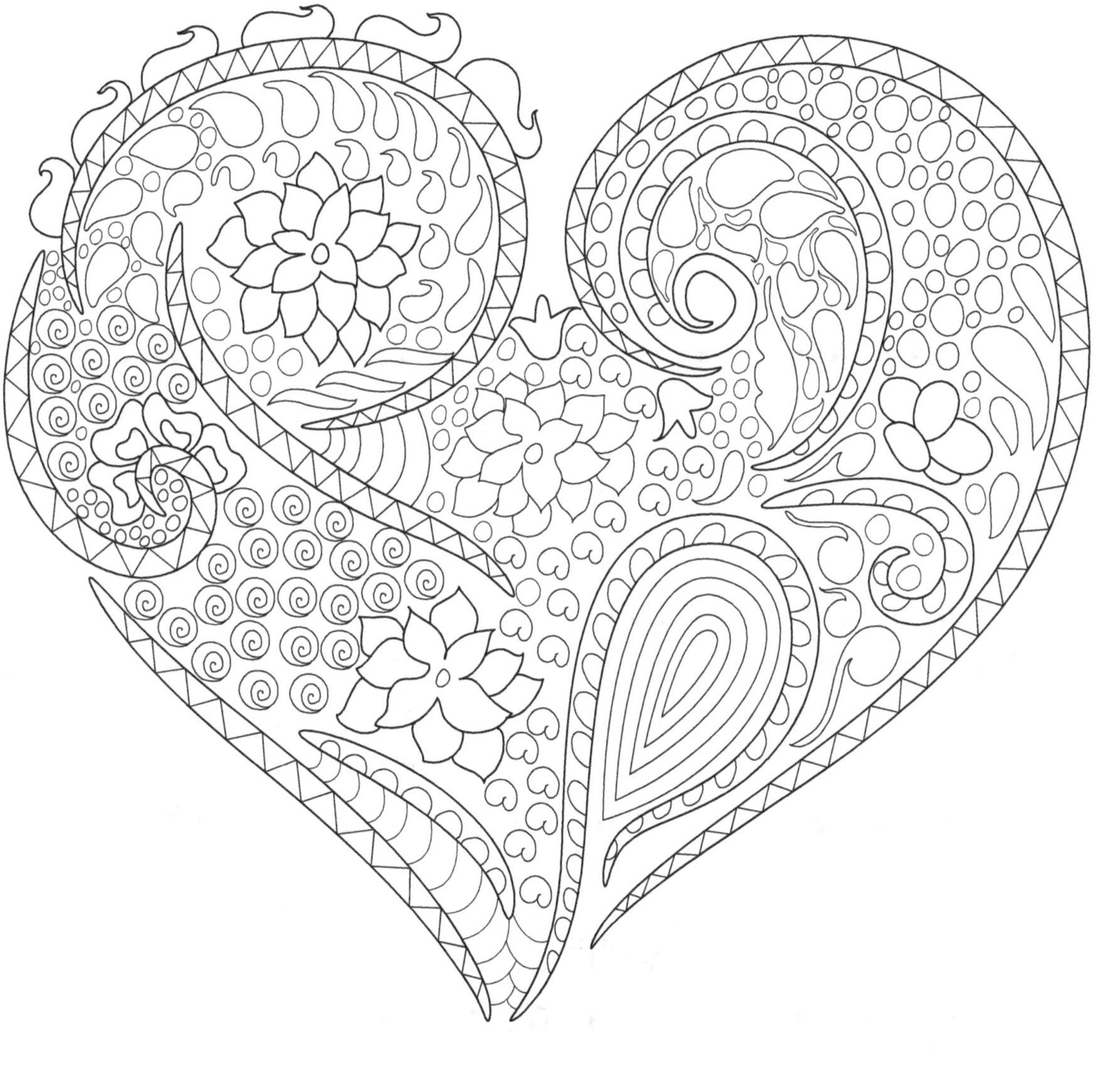

THIS BOOK BELONGS TO
MY BELOVED:

_____

© 2019 Queen Press. All rights reserved.

This book or parts thereof may not be reproduced in any form, stored in any retrieval system, or transmitted in any form by any means — electronic, mechanical, photocopy, recording, or otherwise — without prior written permission of the publisher, except as provided by United States of America copyright law.

Visit us at:
www.amazon.com/author/queenpress

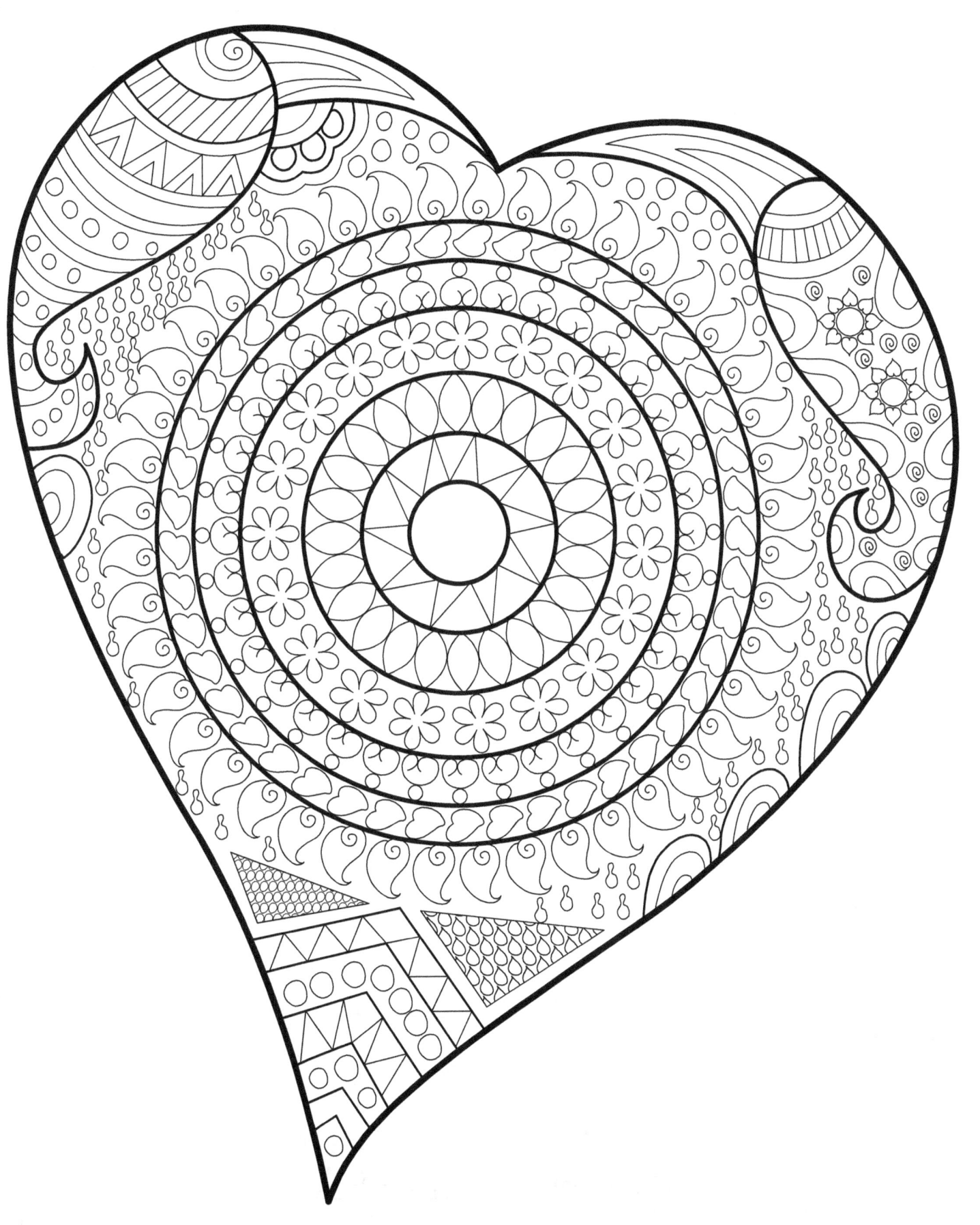

Copyright © Queen Press

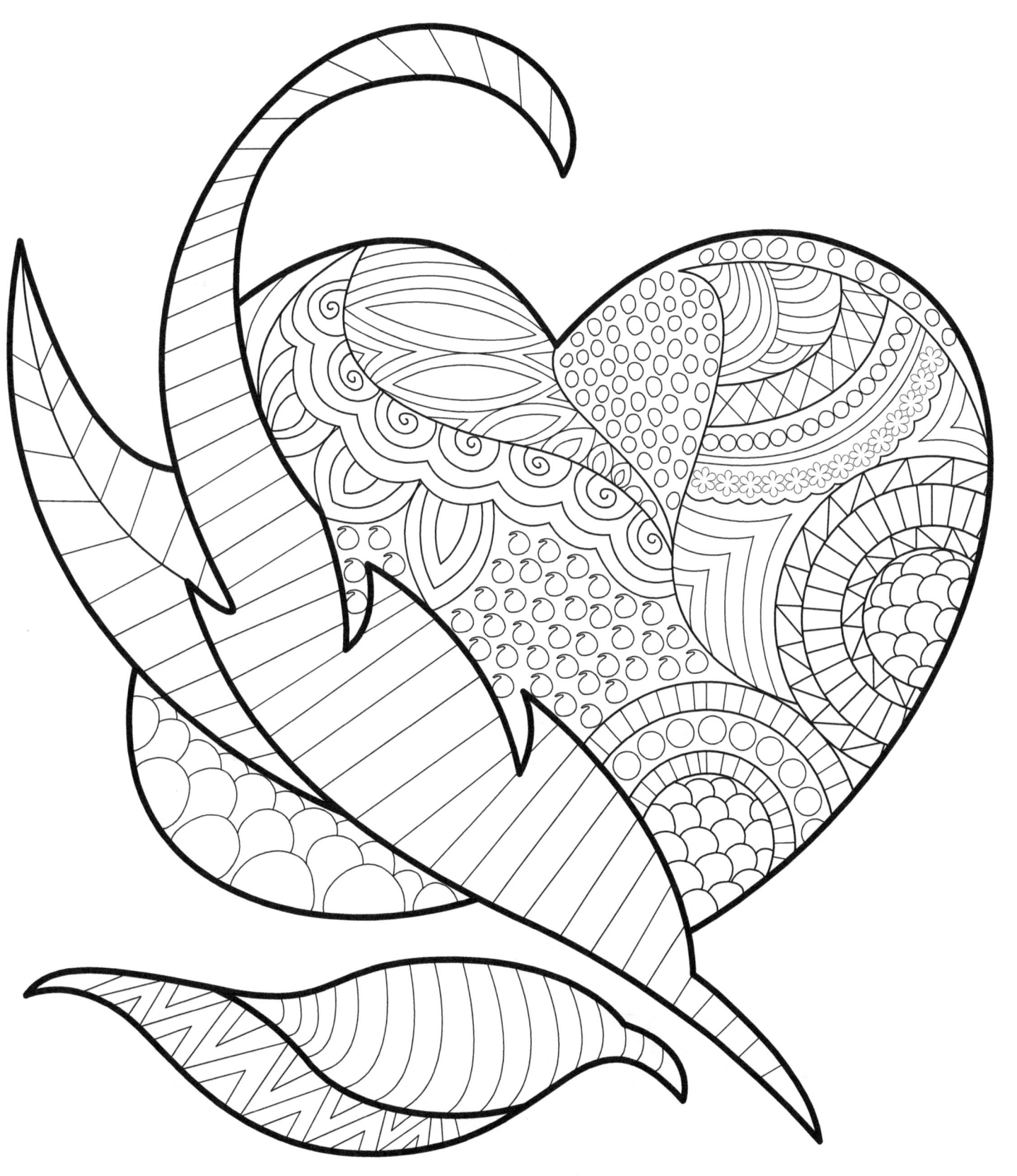

Copyright © Queen Press

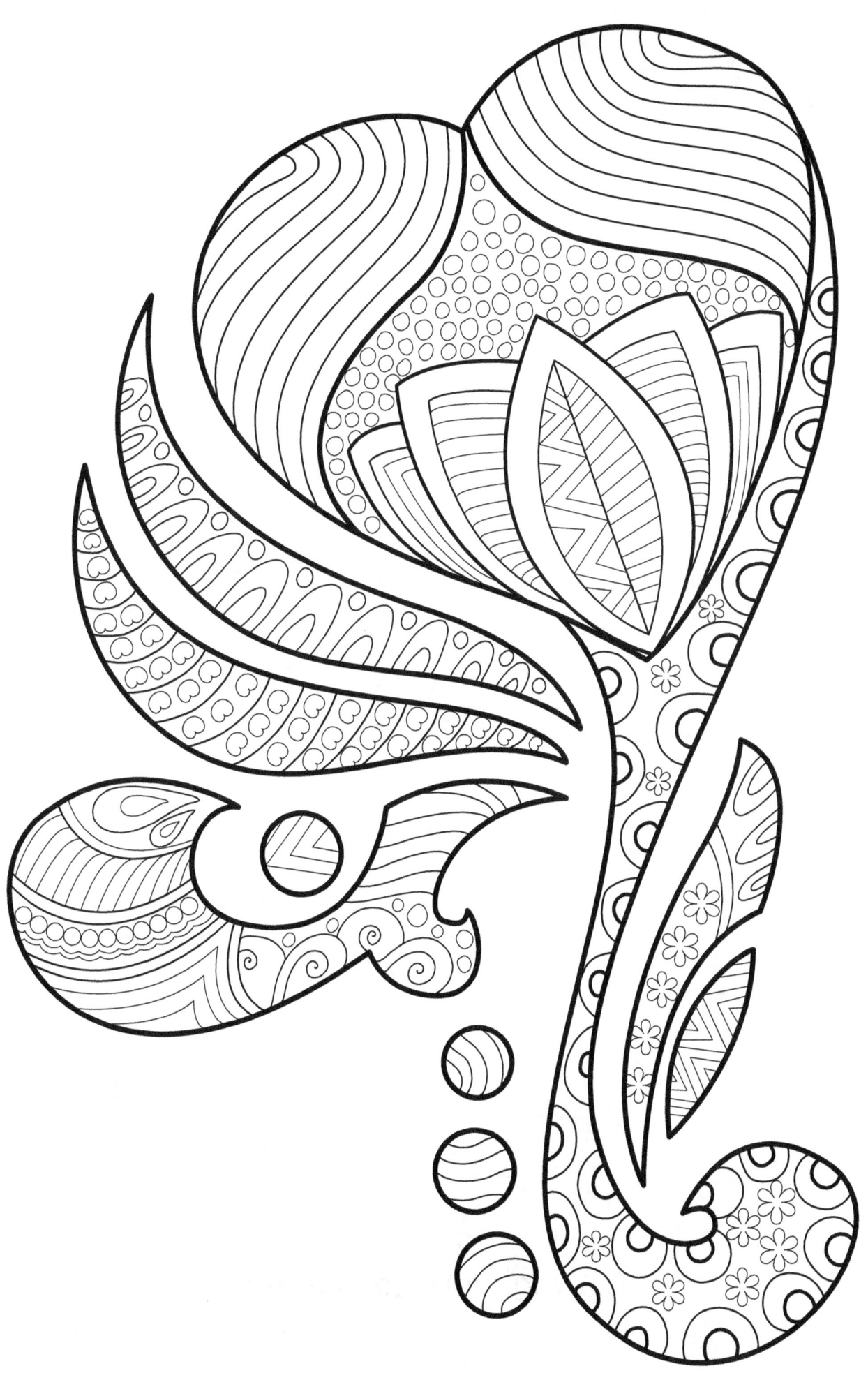

Copyright © Queen Press

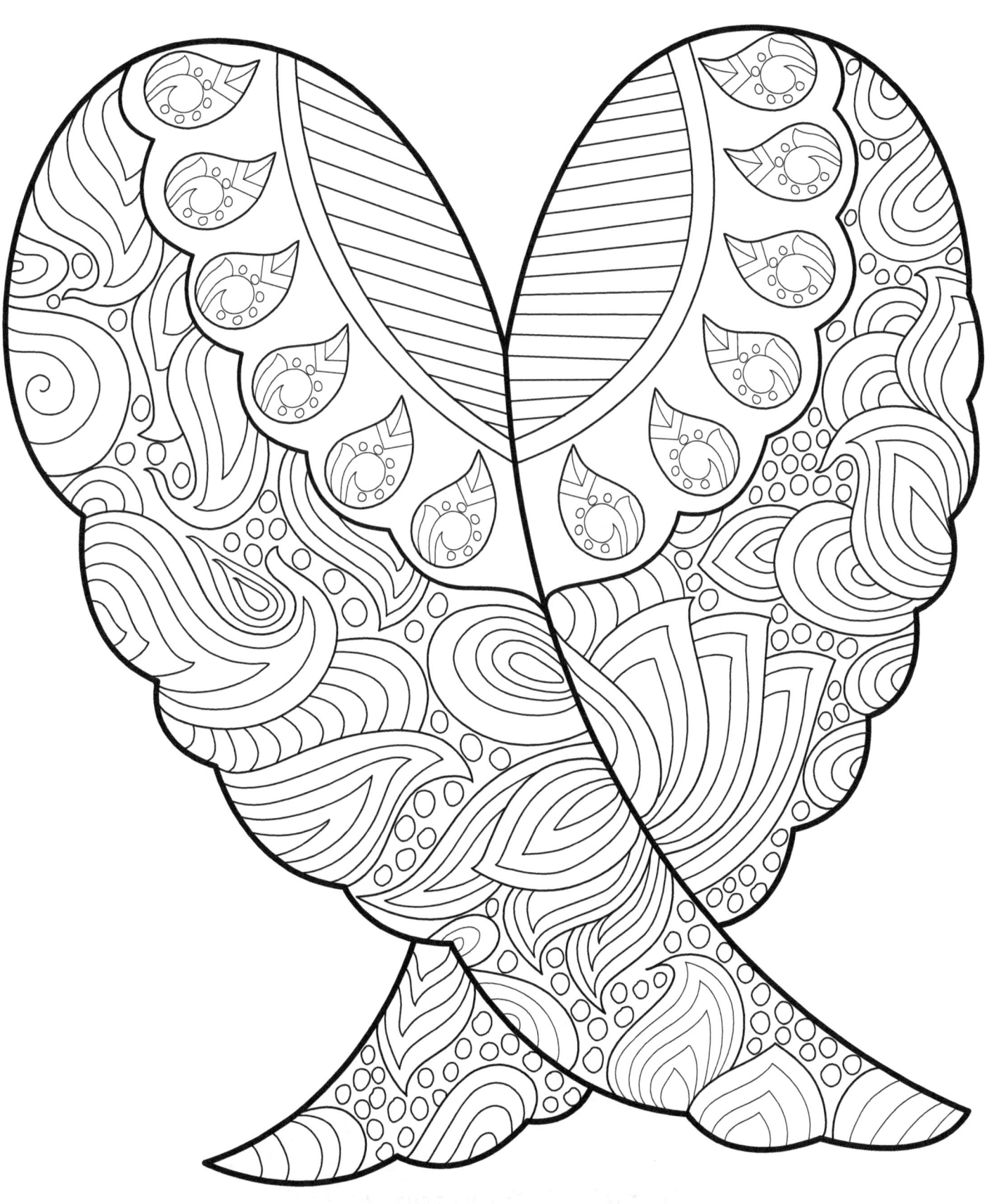

Copyright © Queen Press

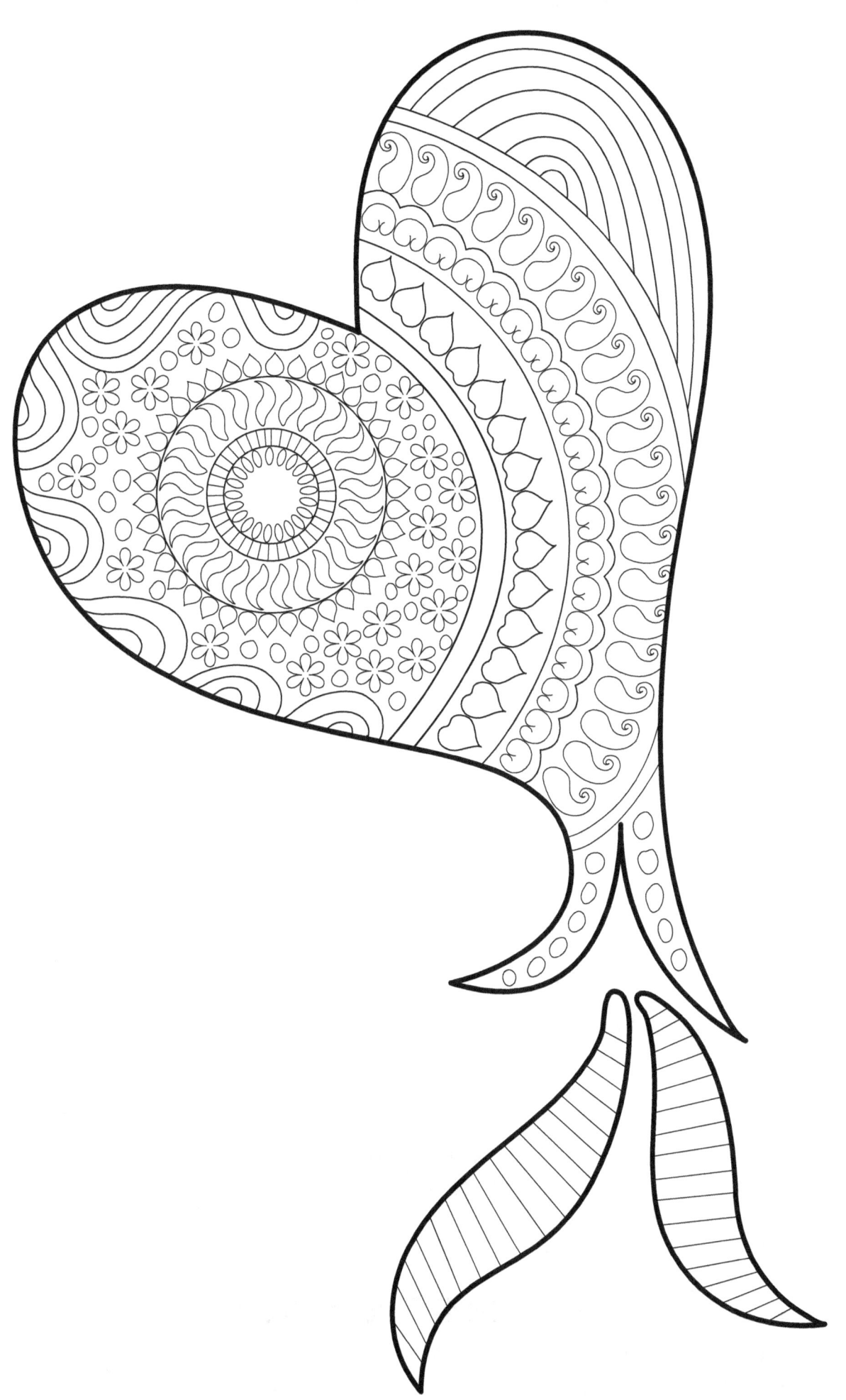

Copyright © Queen Press

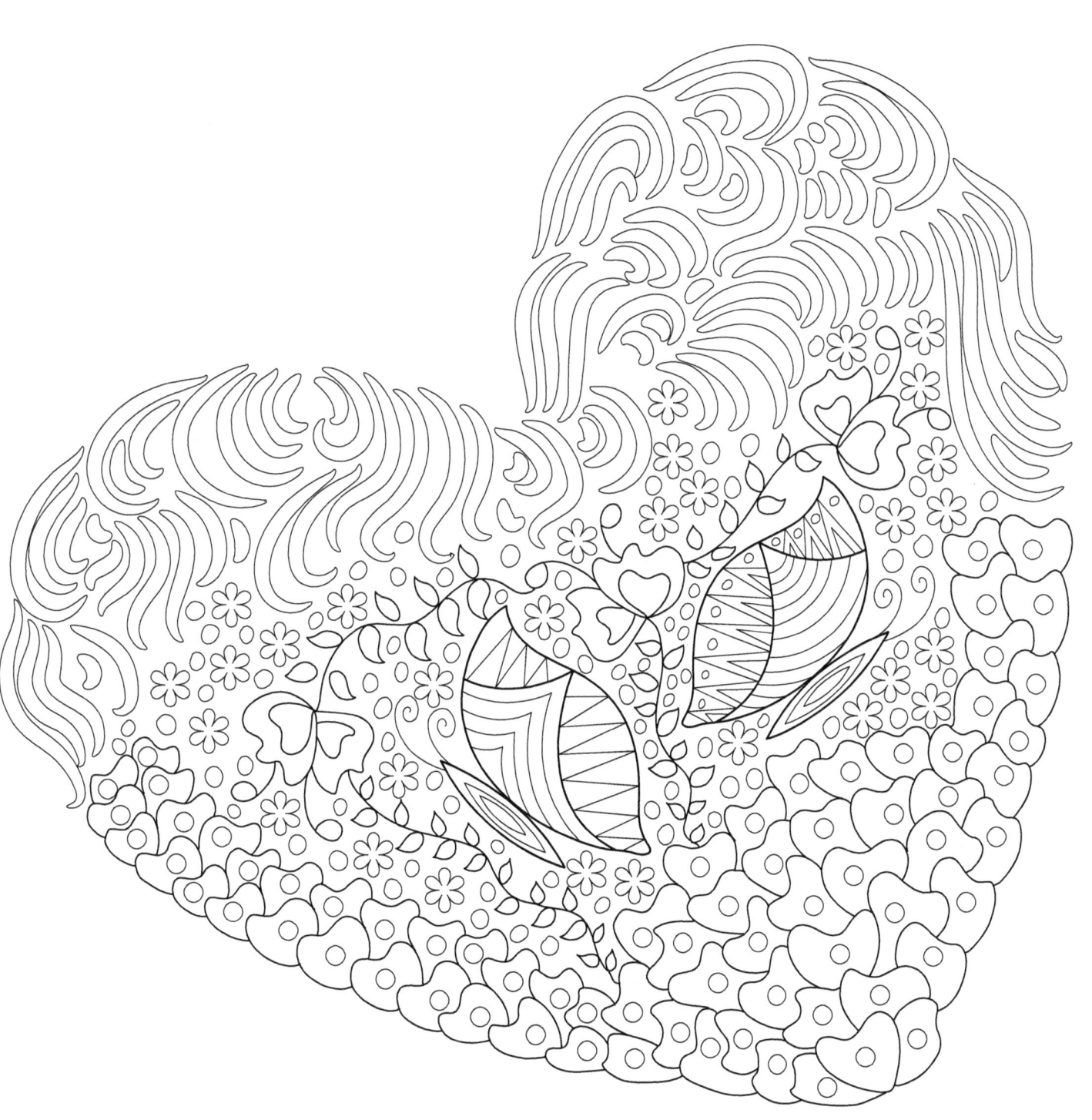

Copyright © Queen Press

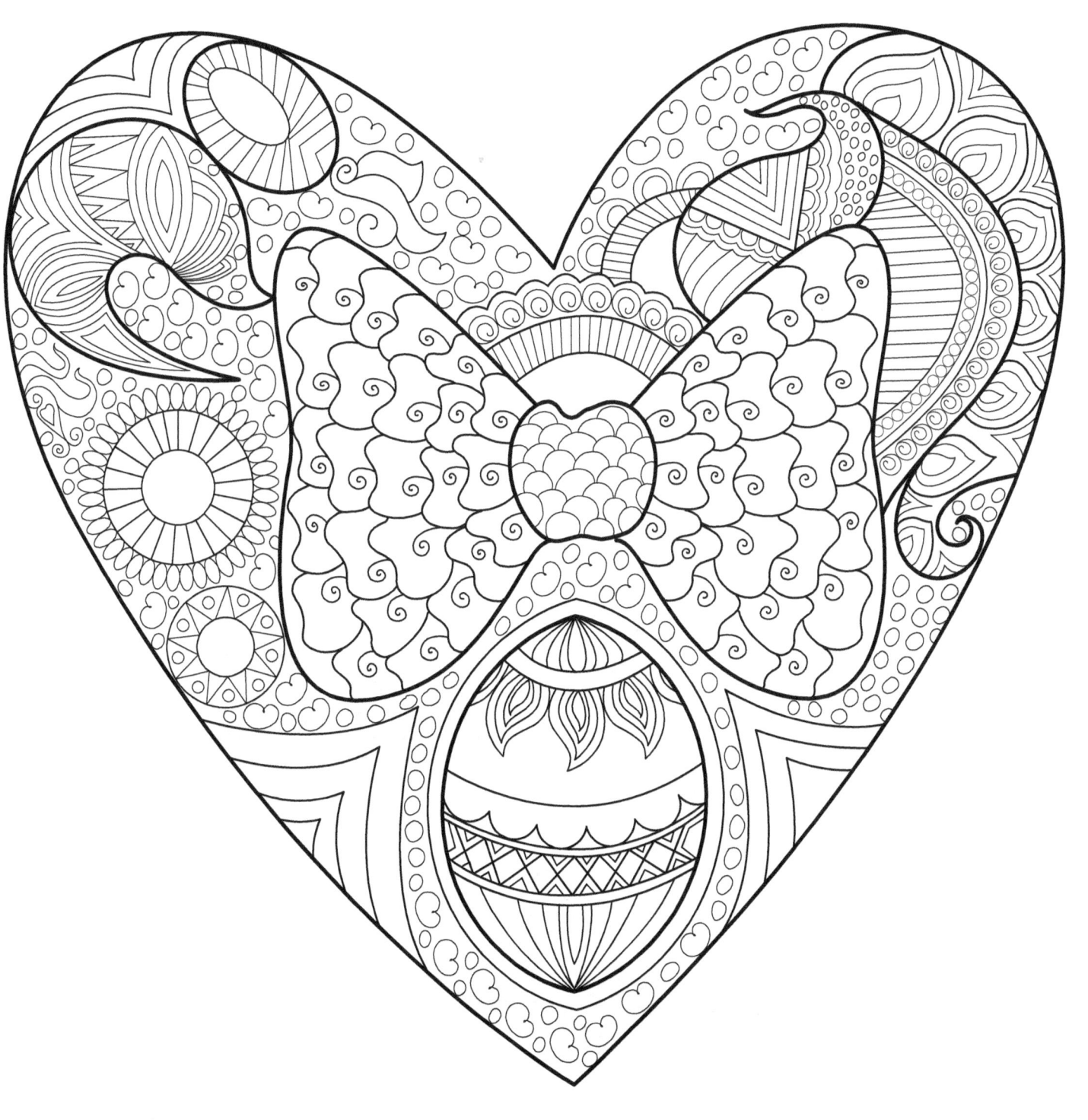

Copyright © Queen Press

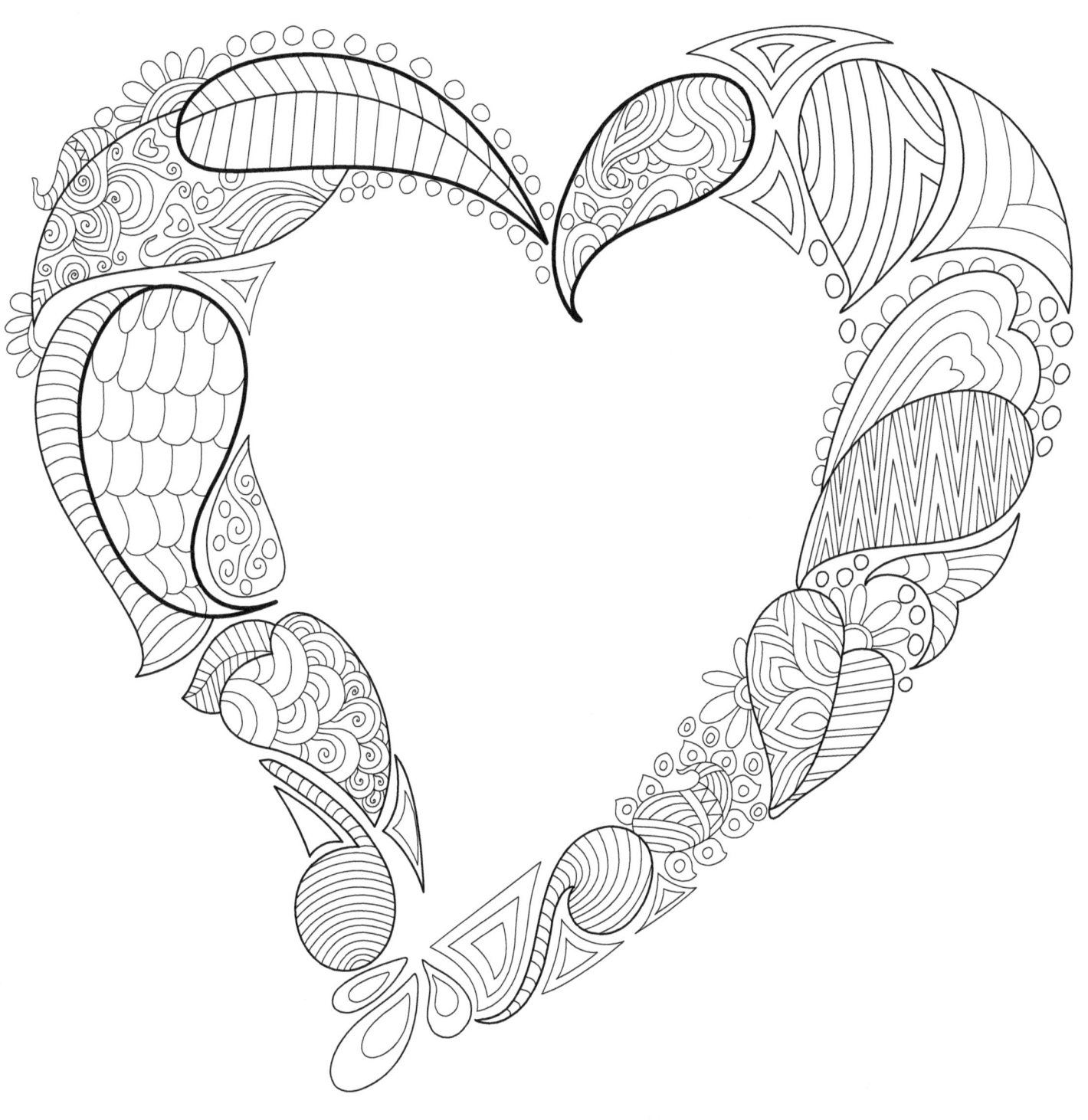

Copyright © Queen Press

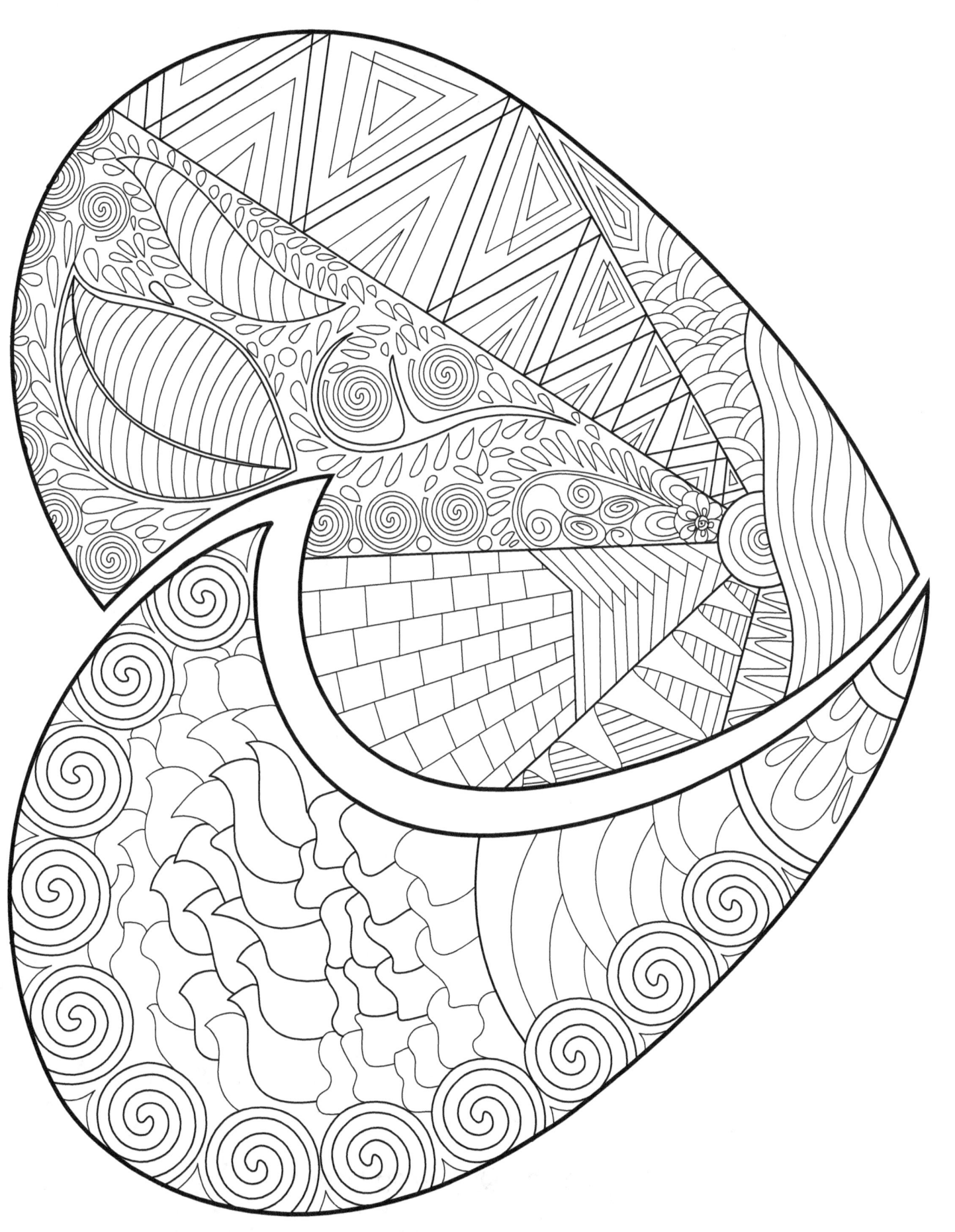

Copyright © Queen Press

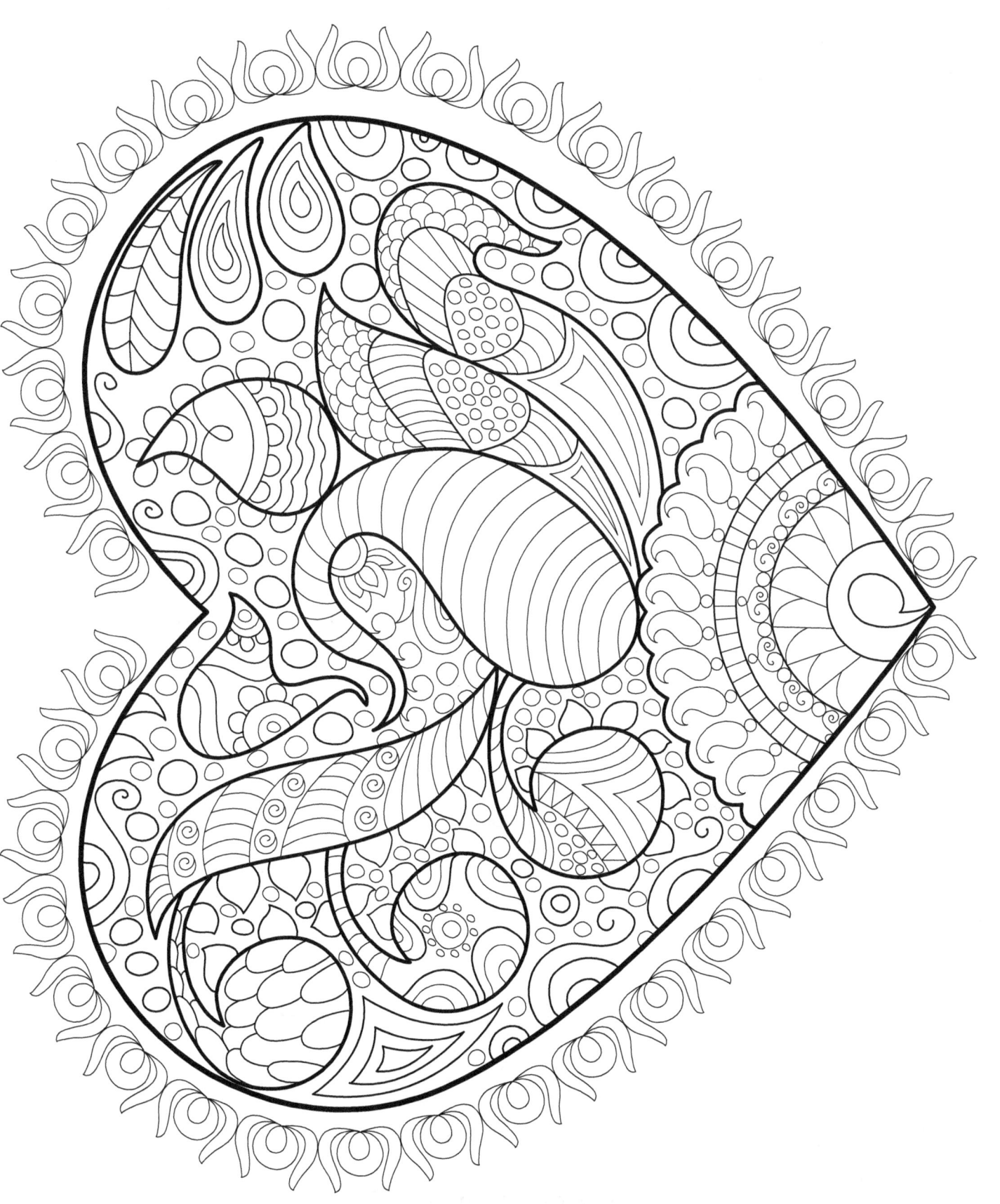

Copyright © Queen Press

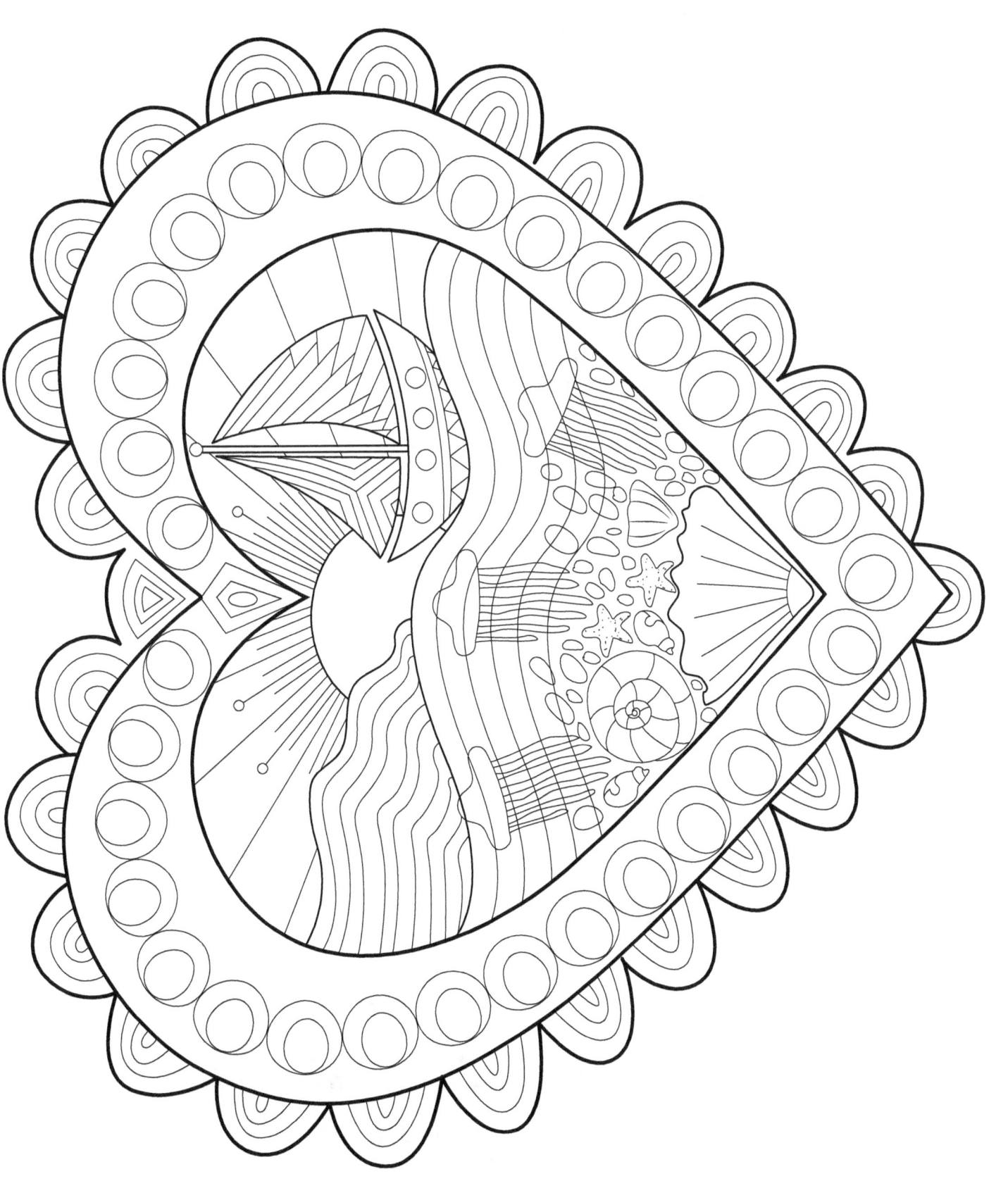

Copyright © Queen Press

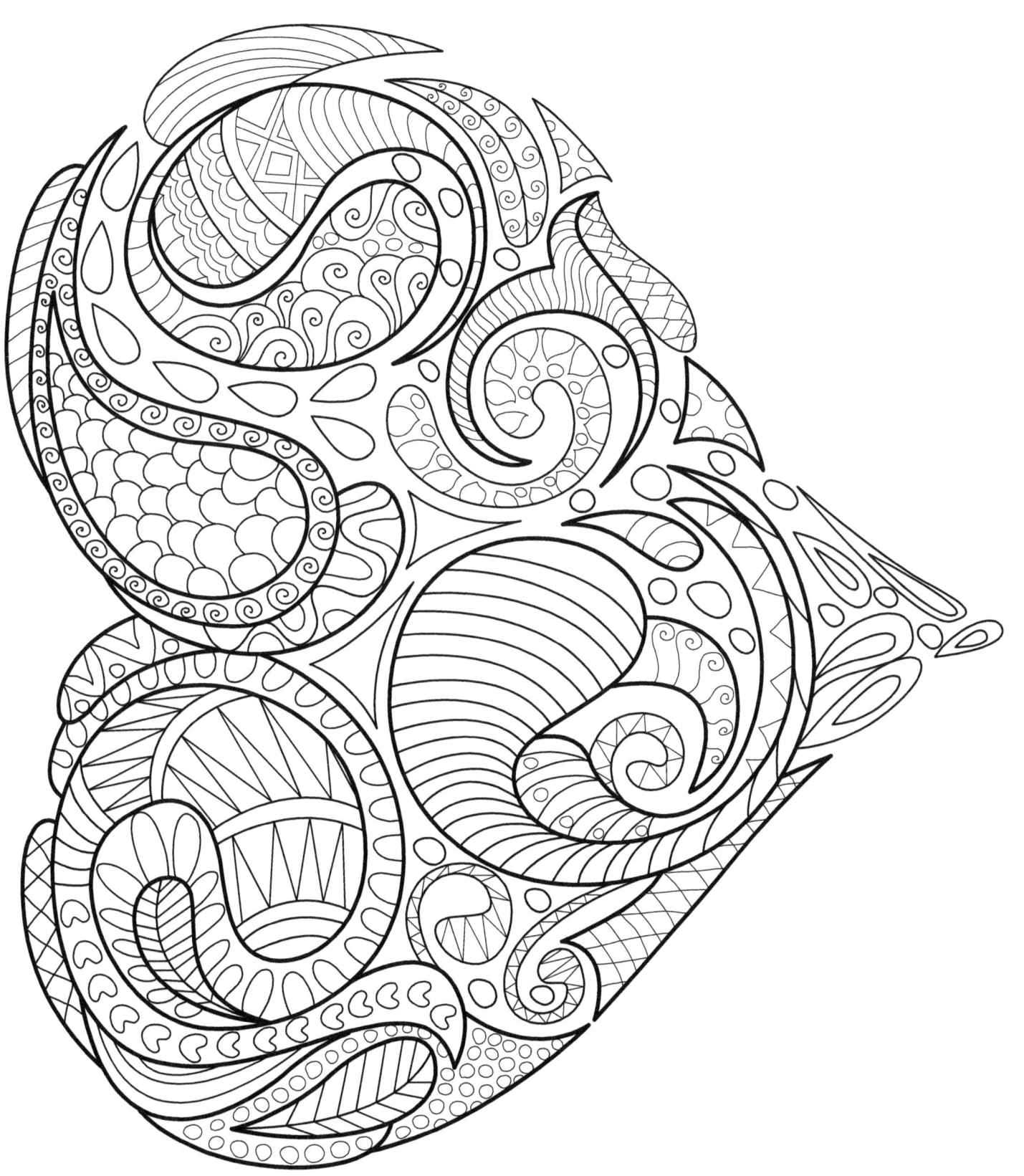

Copyright © Queen Press

Copyright © Queen Press

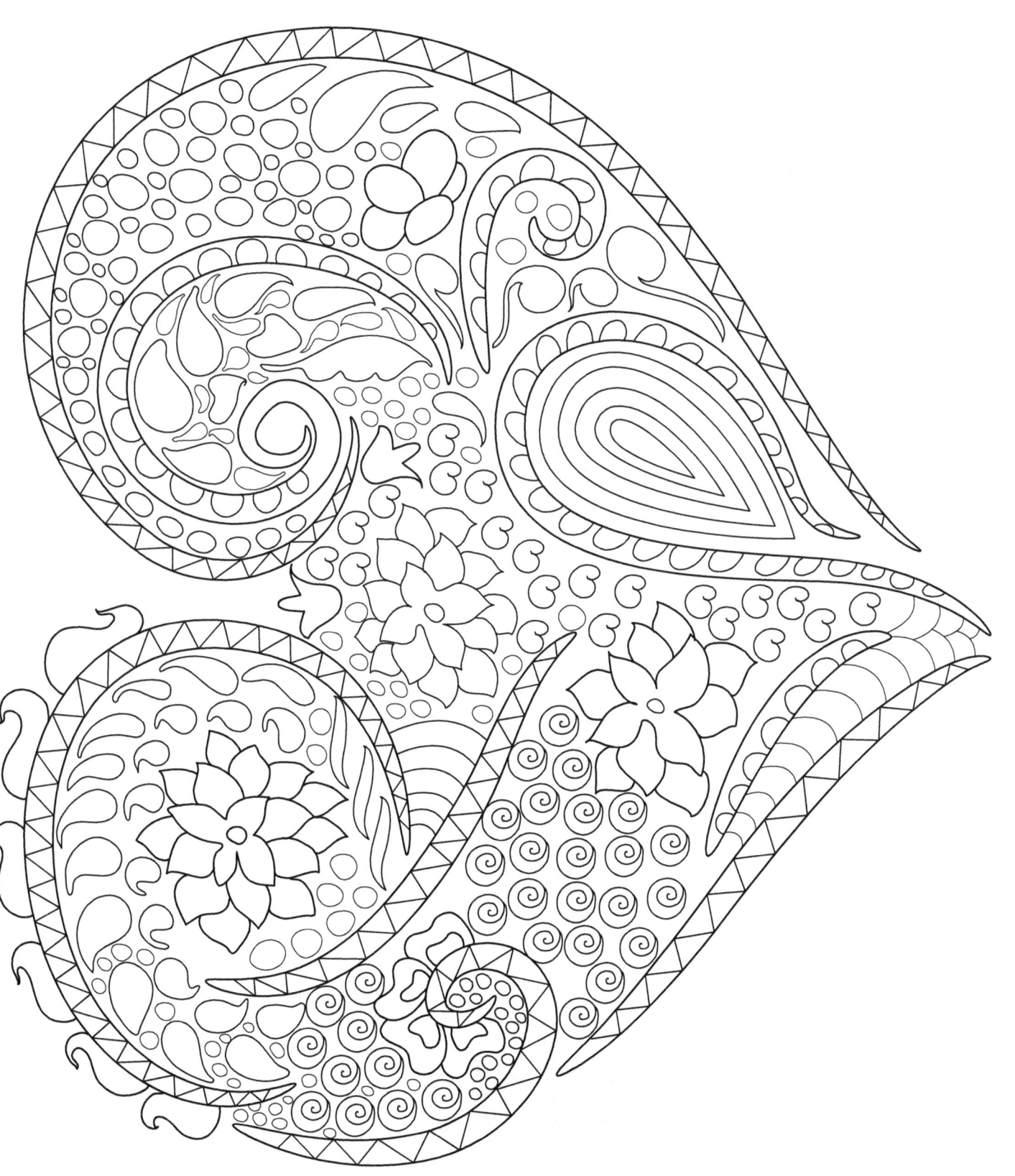

Copyright © Queen Press

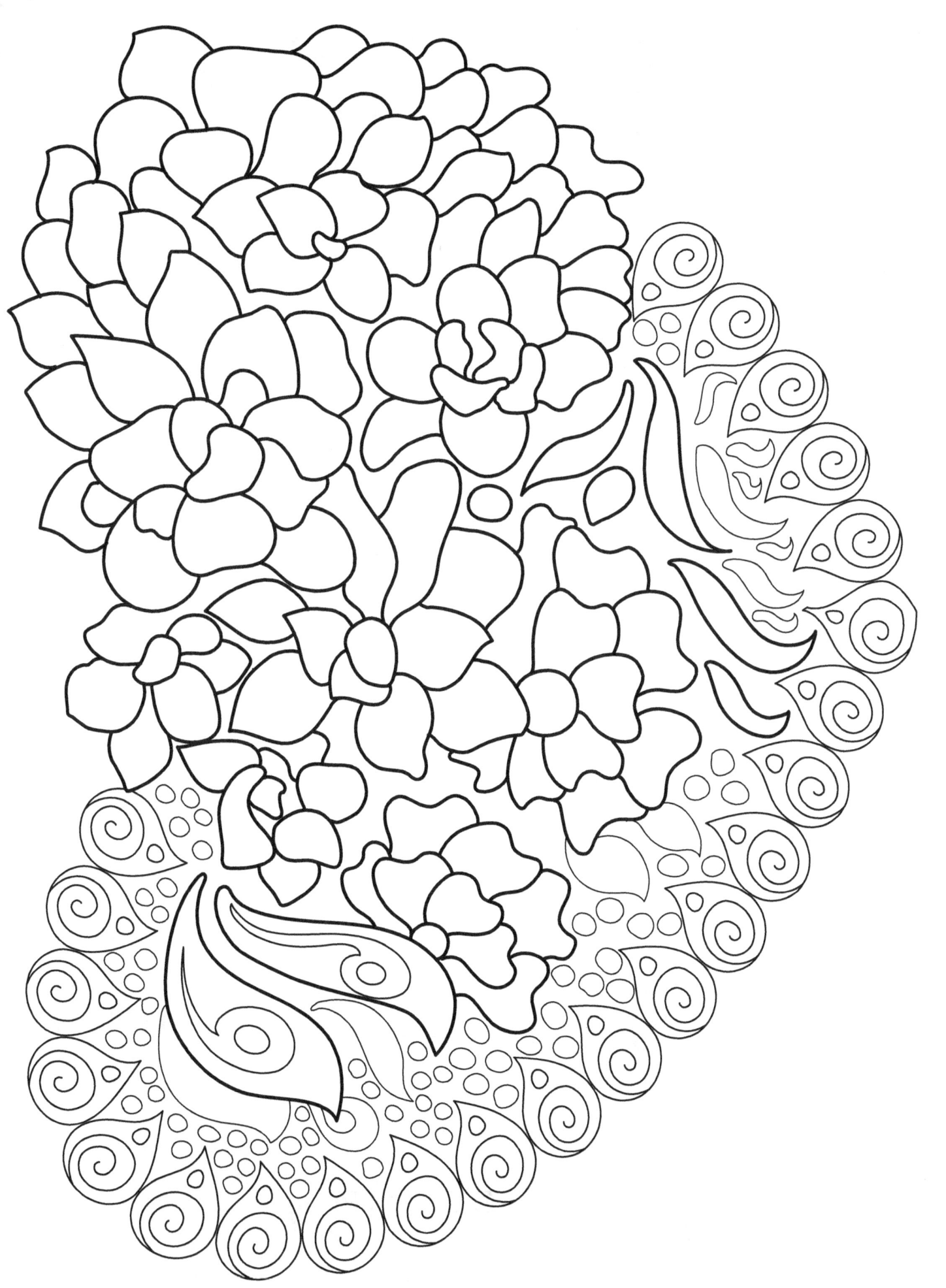

Copyright © Queen Press

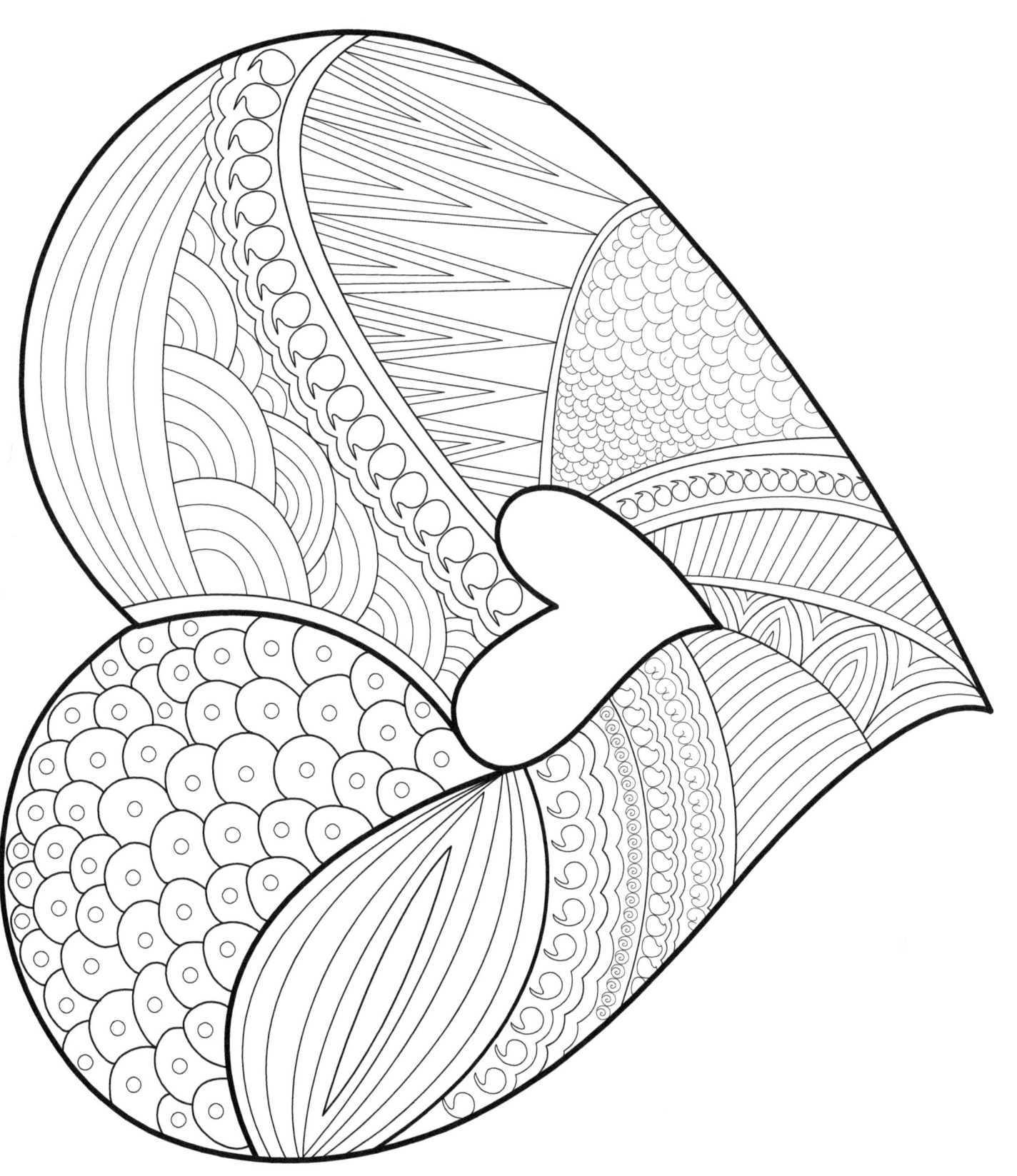

Copyright © Queen Press

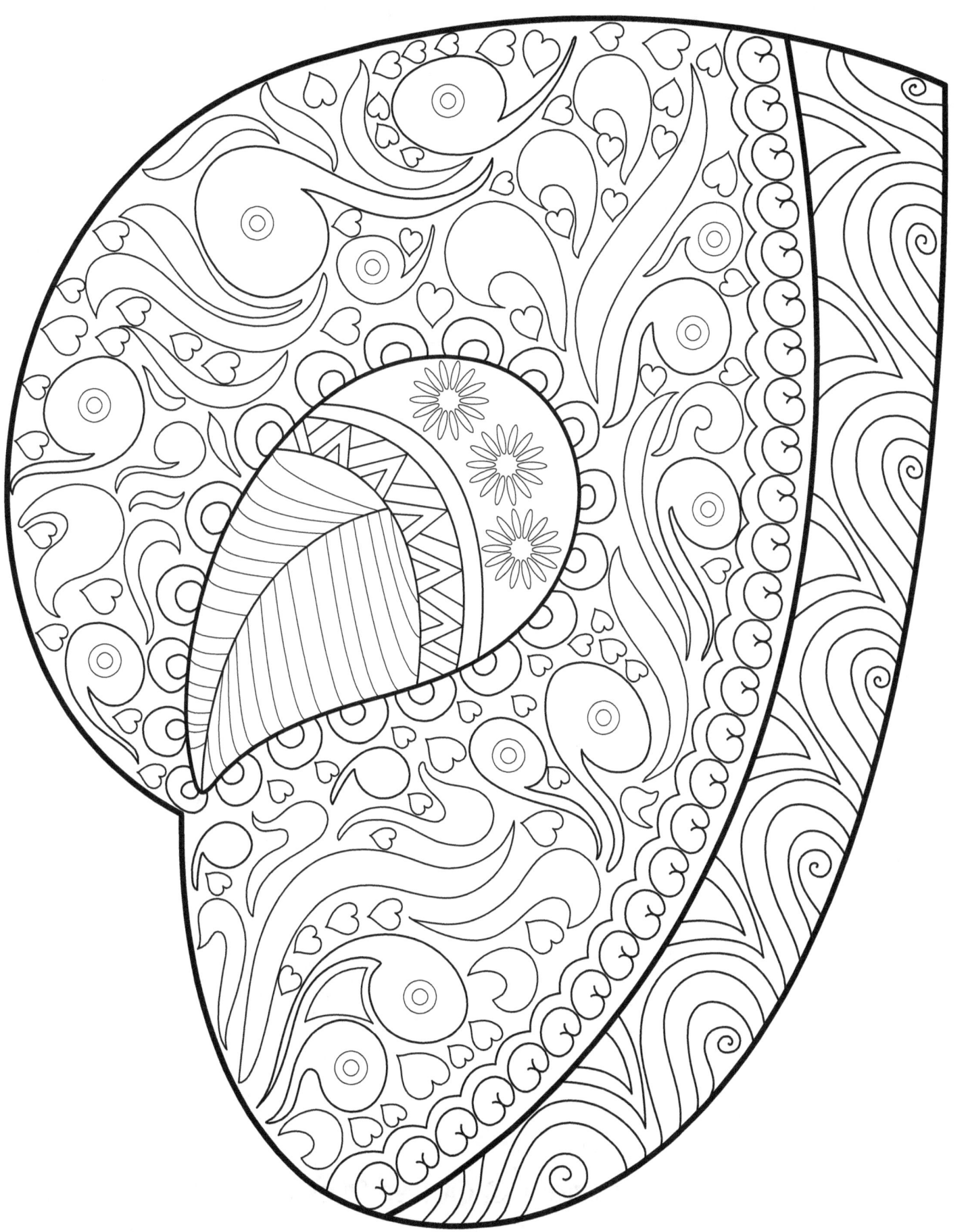

Copyright © Queen Press

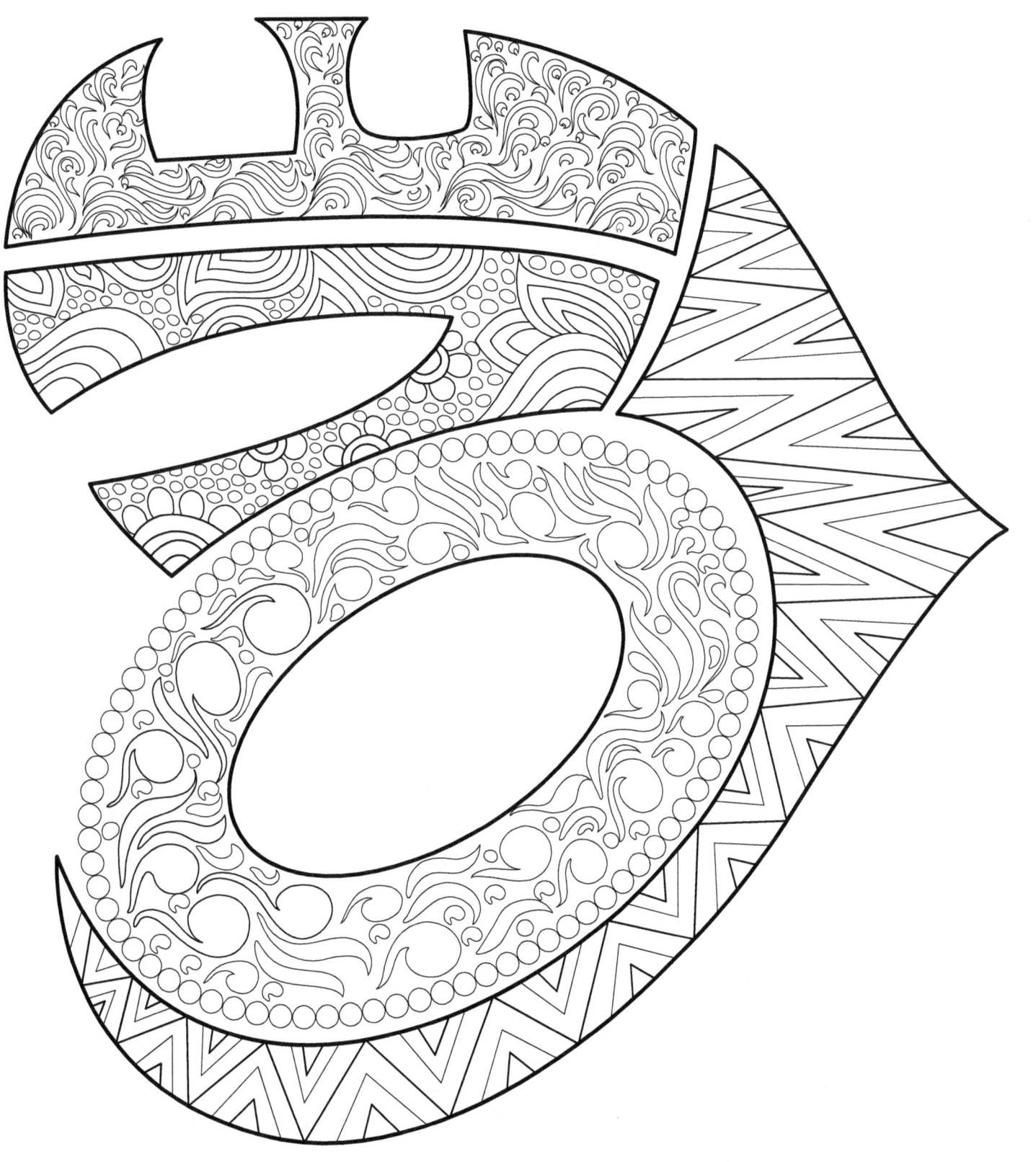

Copyright © Queen Press

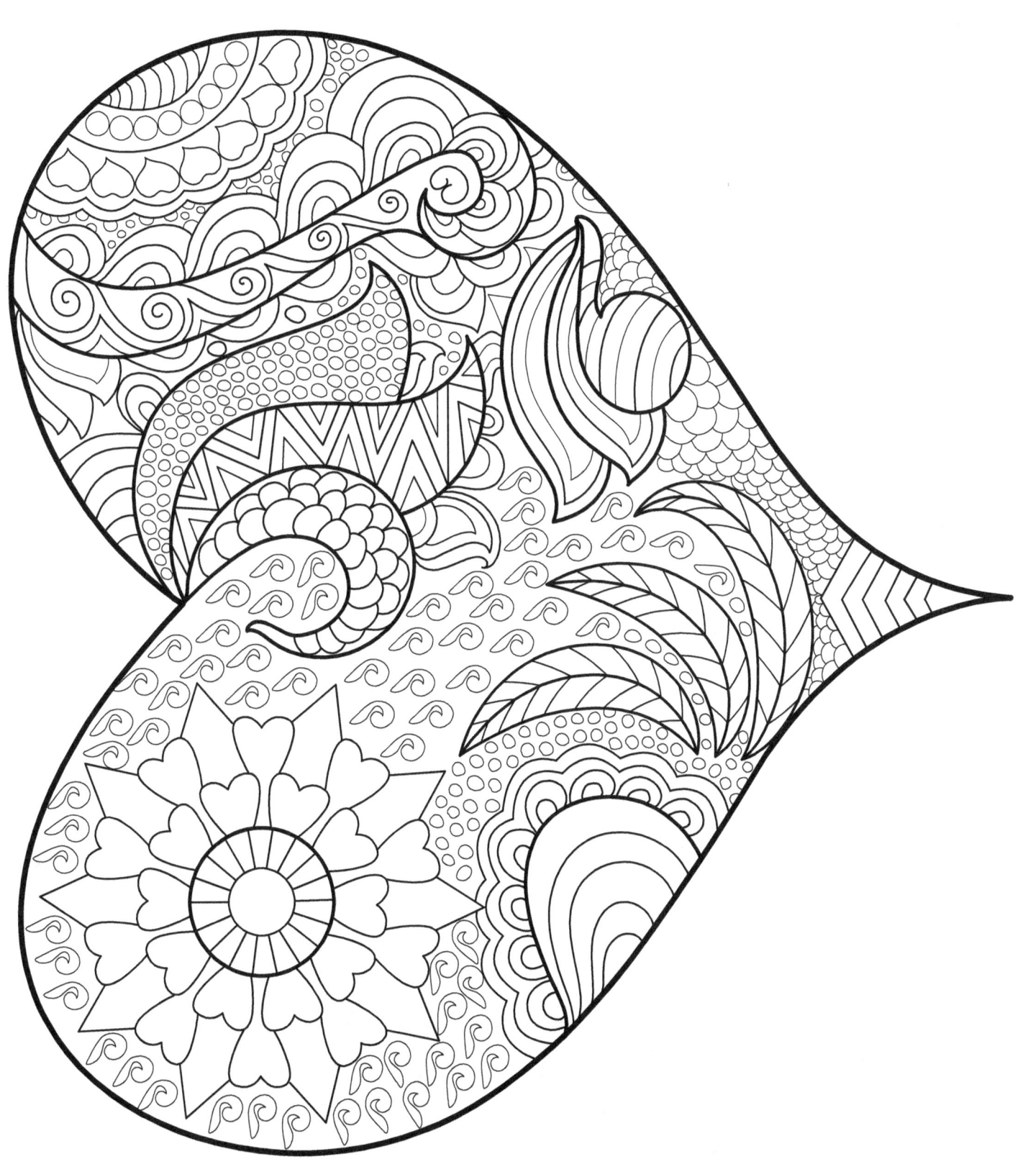

Copyright © Queen Press

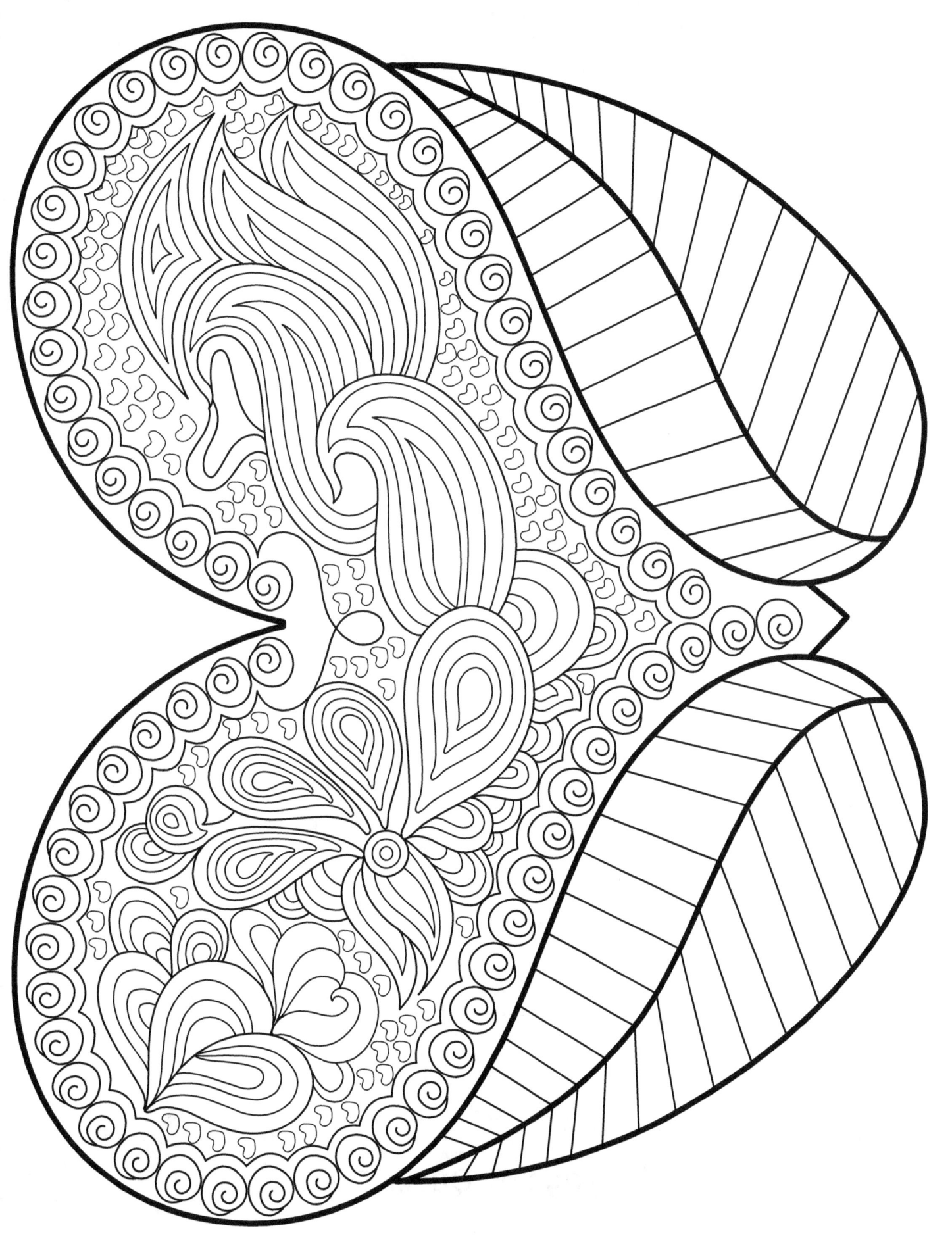

Copyright © Queen Press

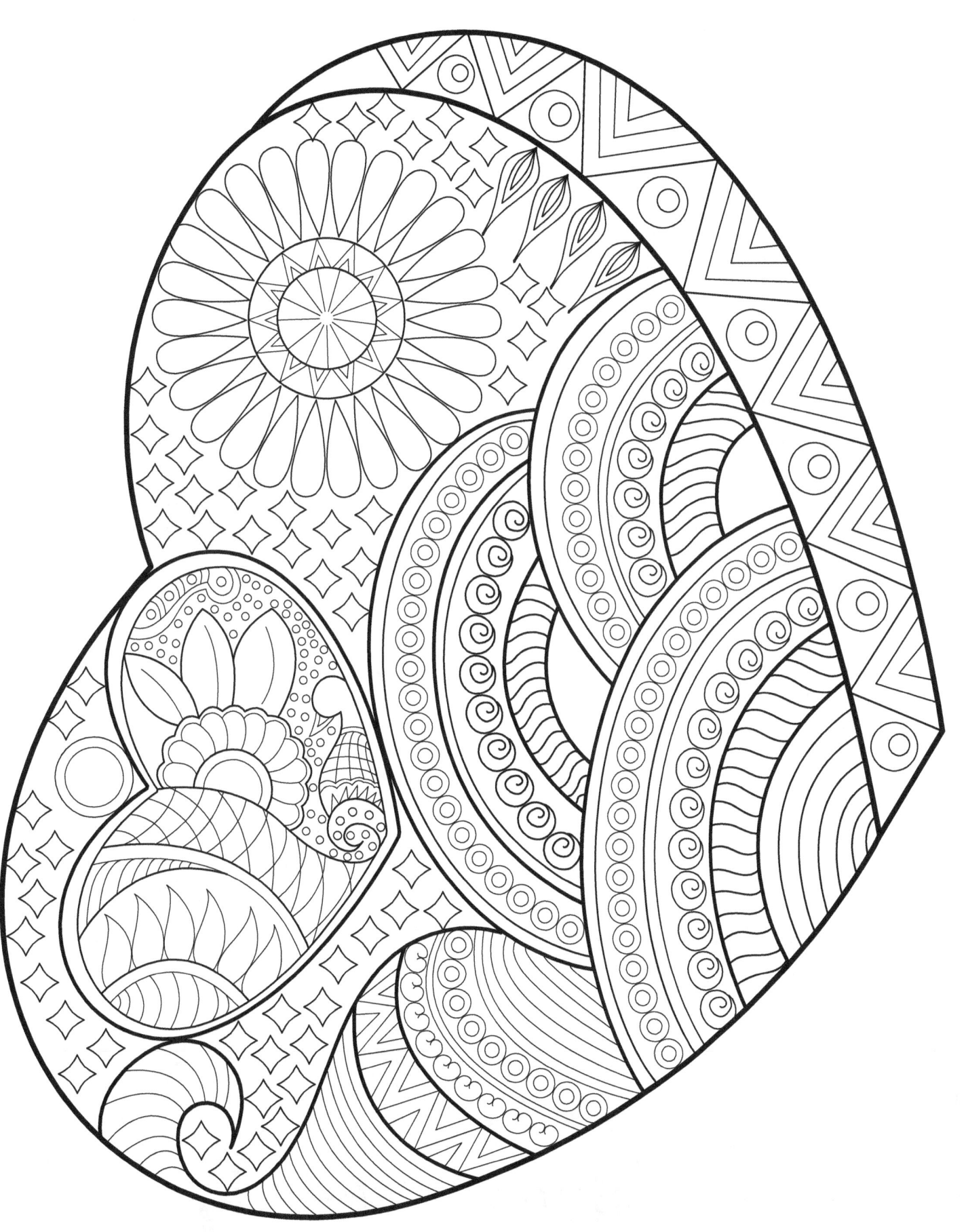

Copyright © Queen Press

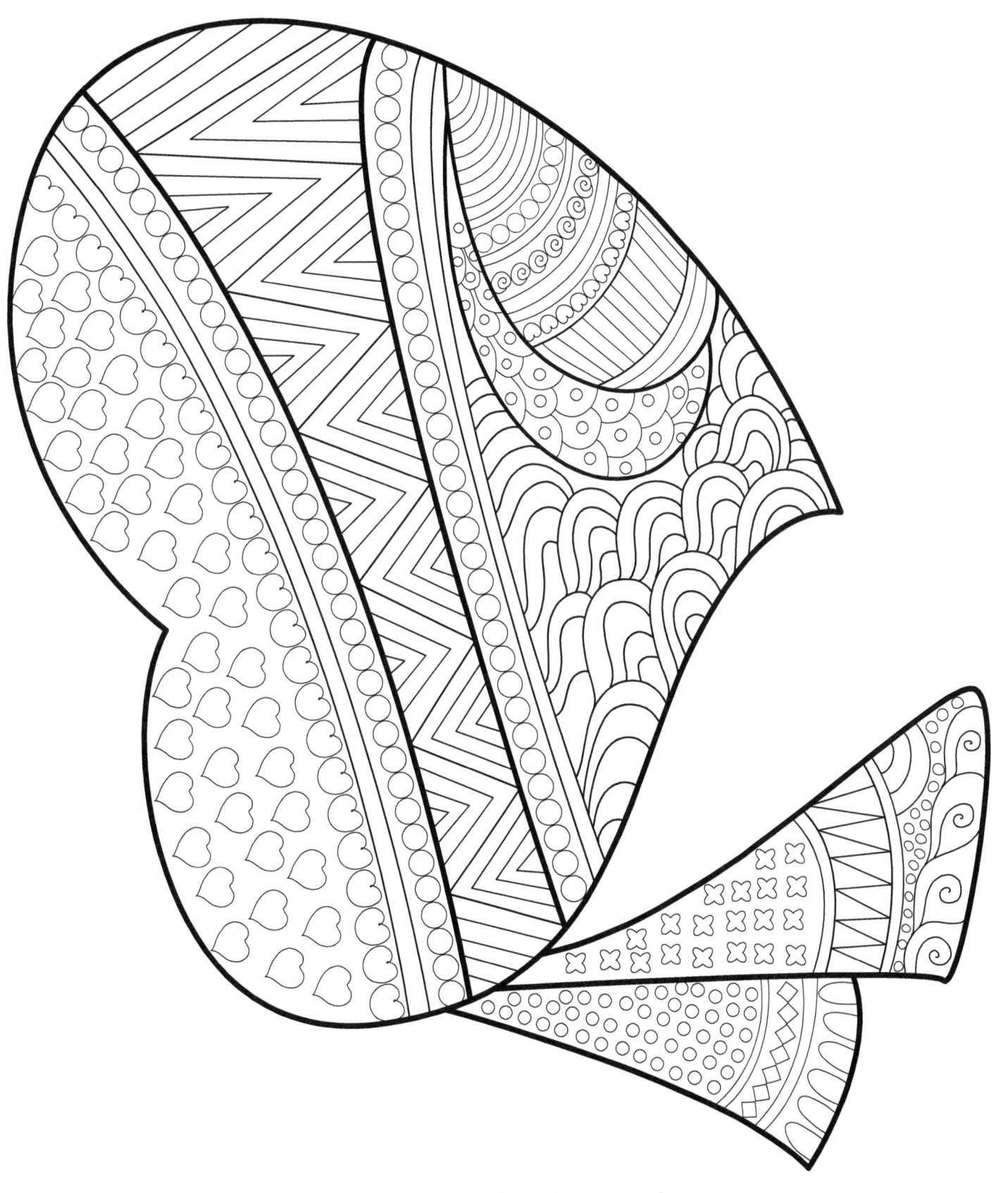

Copyright © Queen Press

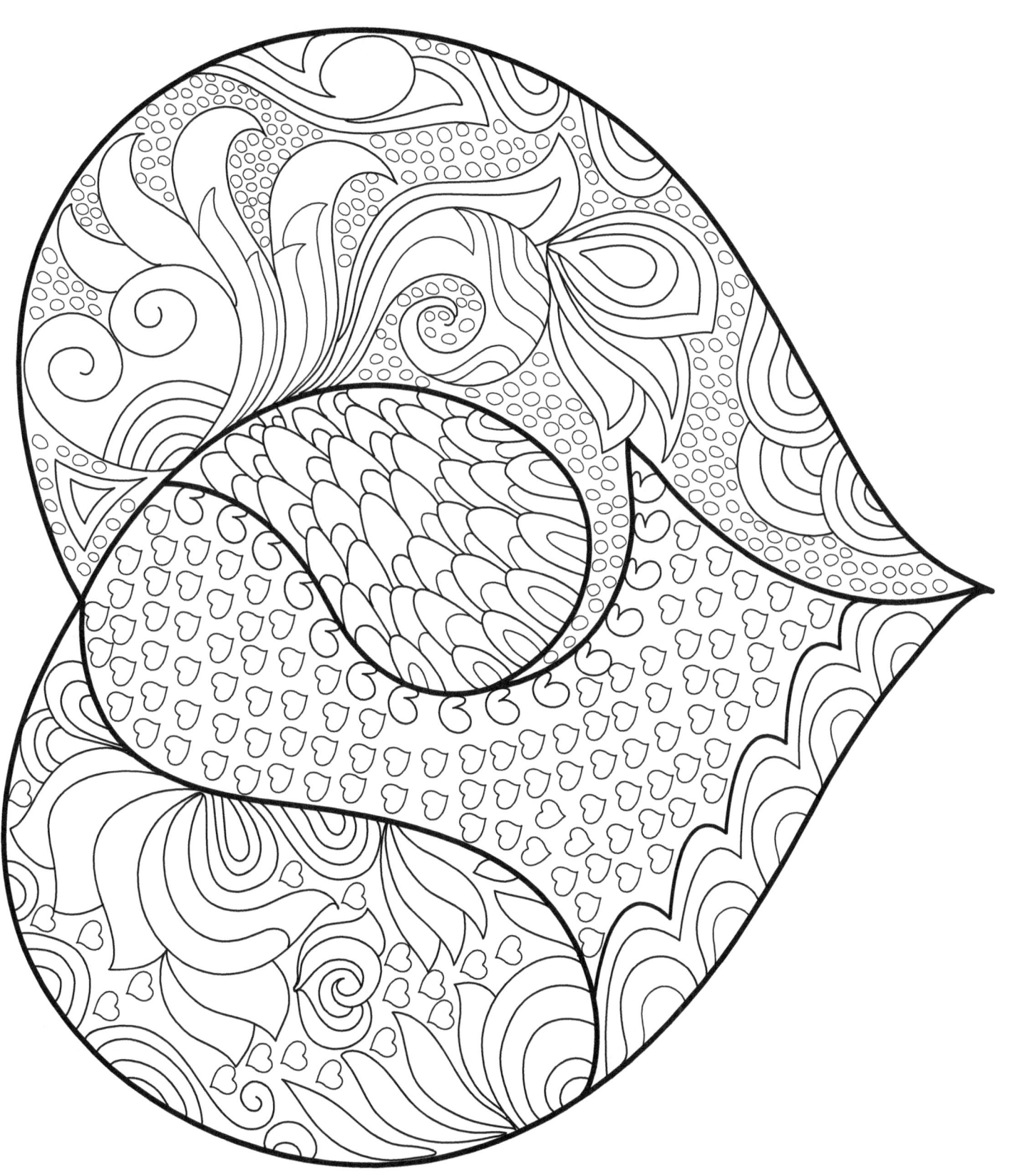

Copyright © Queen Press

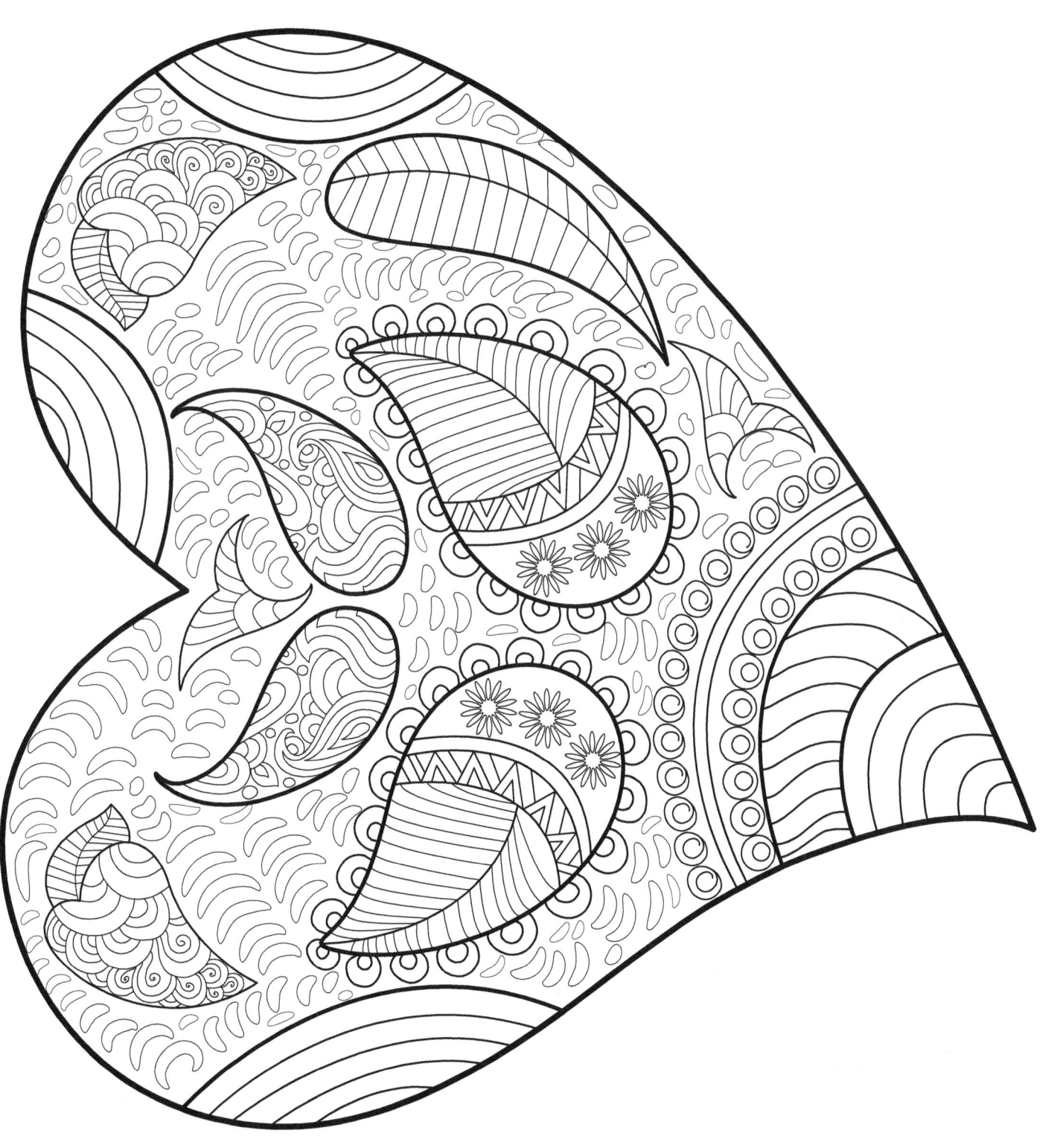

Copyright © Queen Press

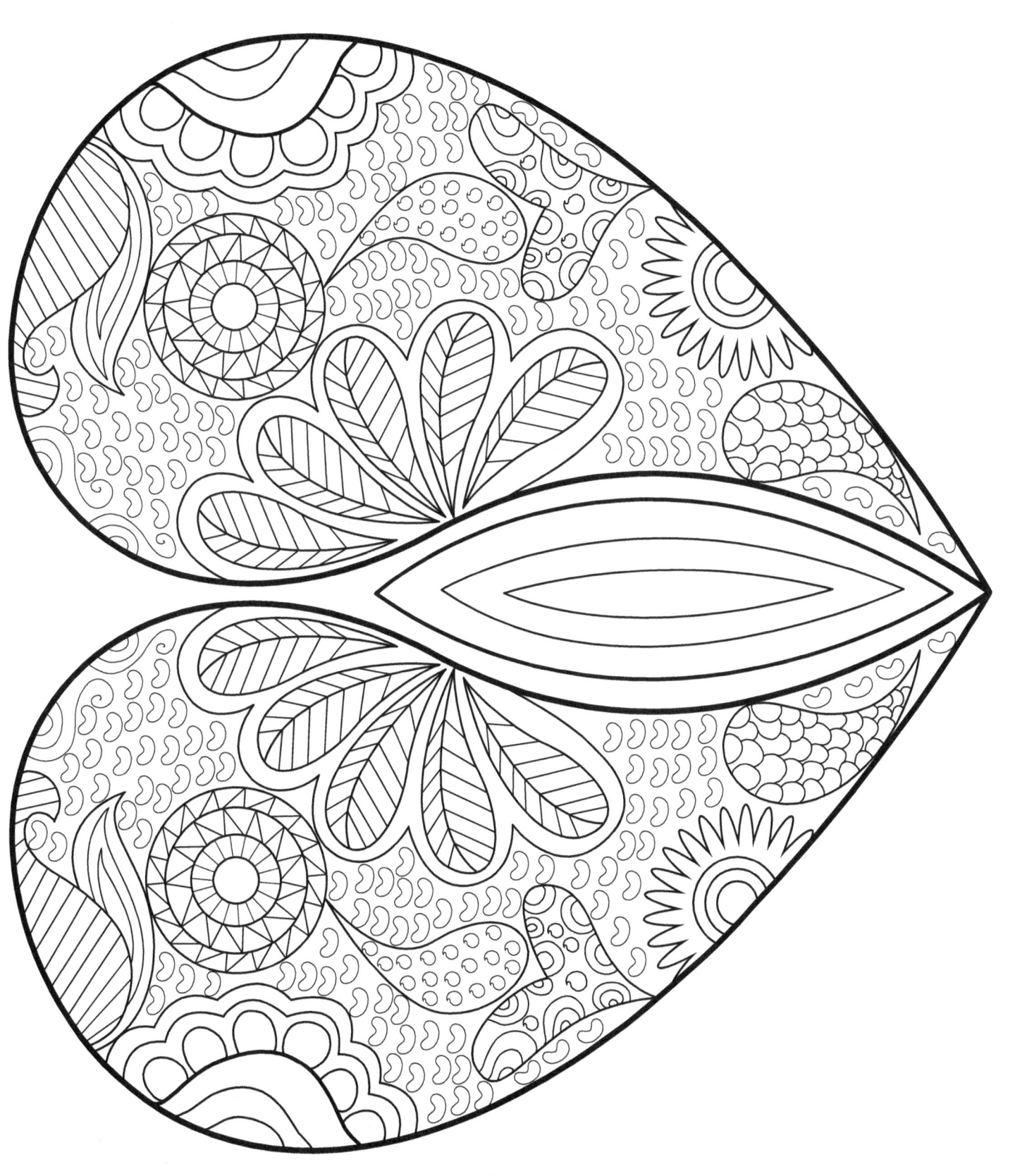

Copyright © Queen Press

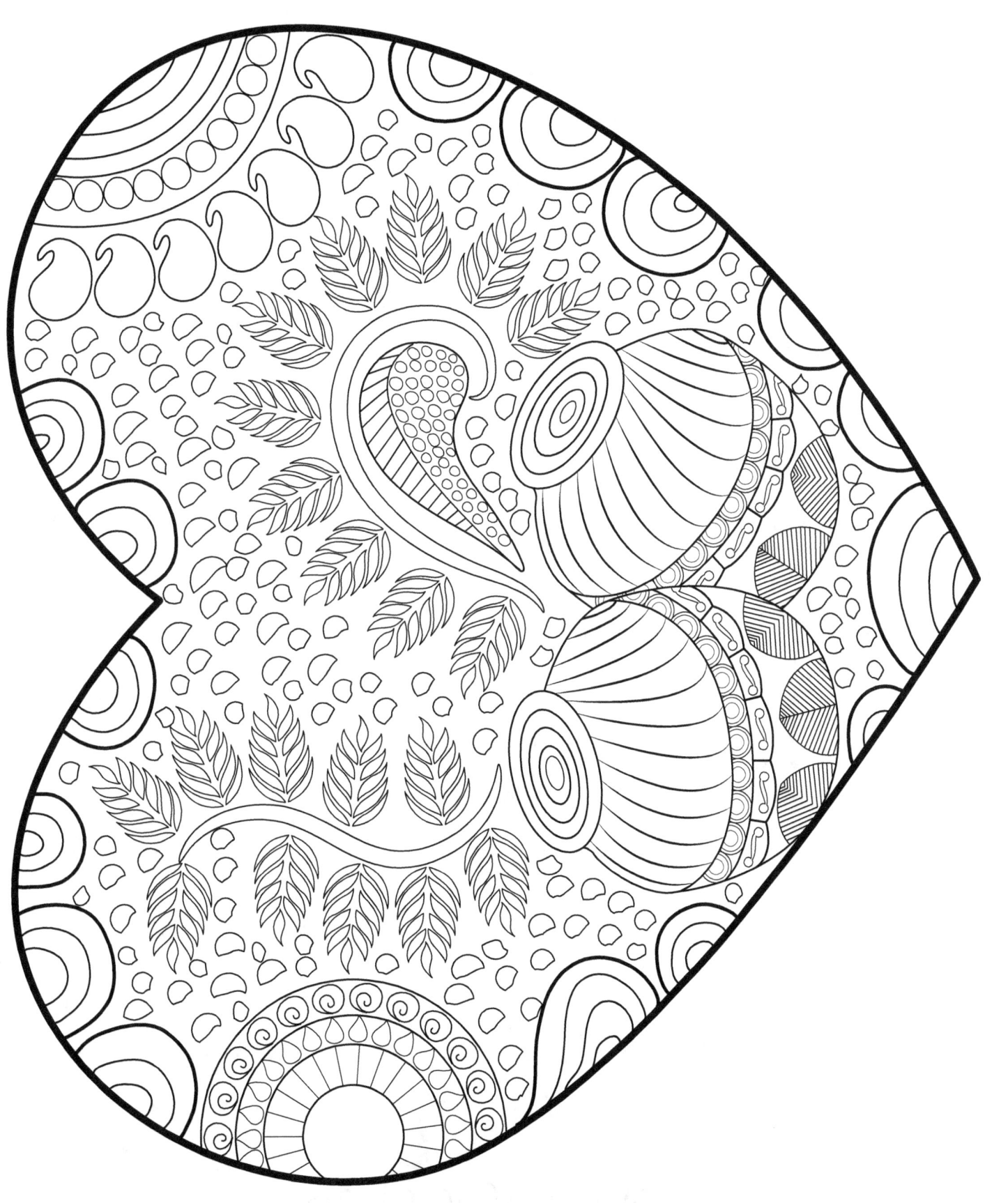

Copyright © Queen Press

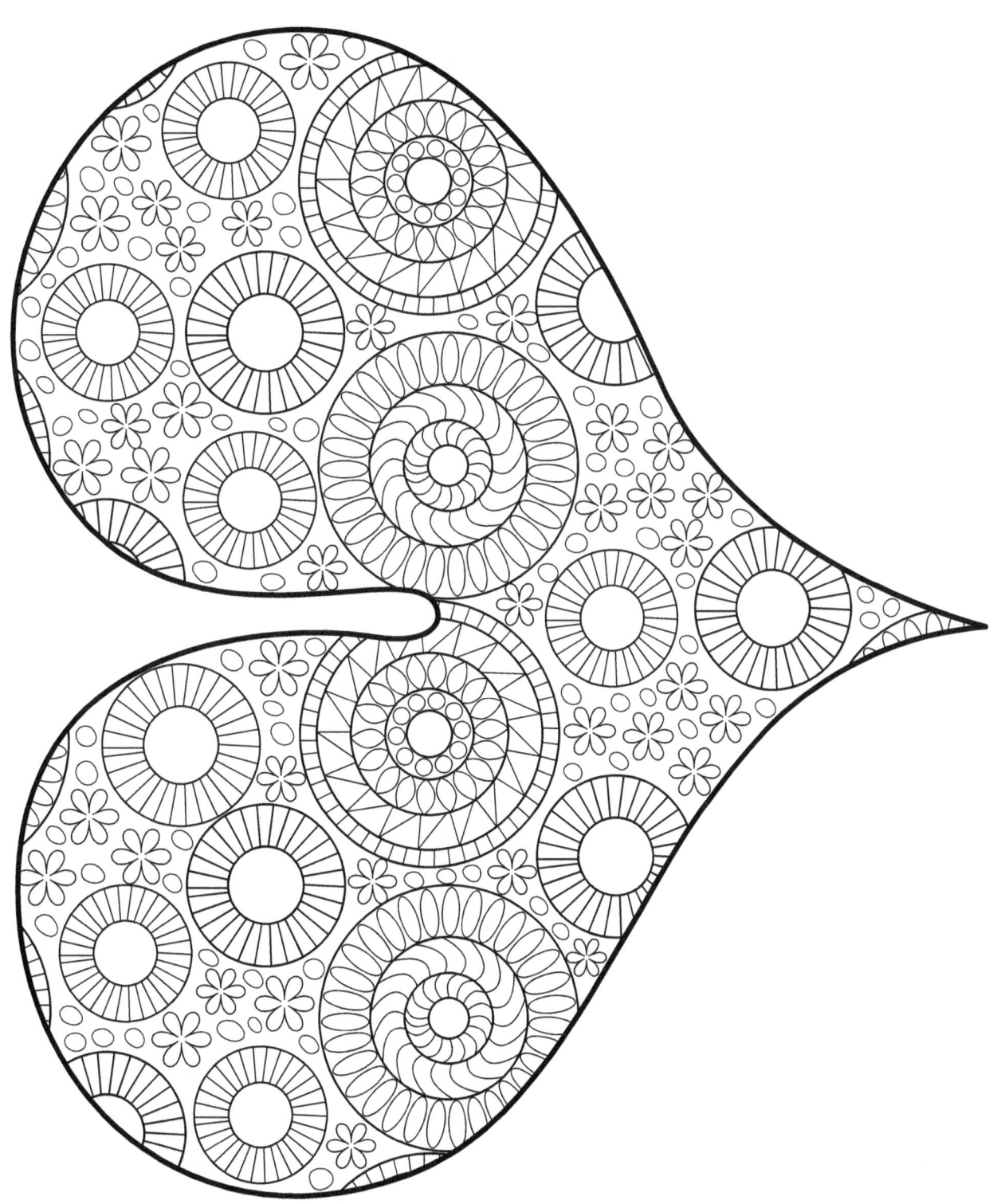

Copyright © Queen Press

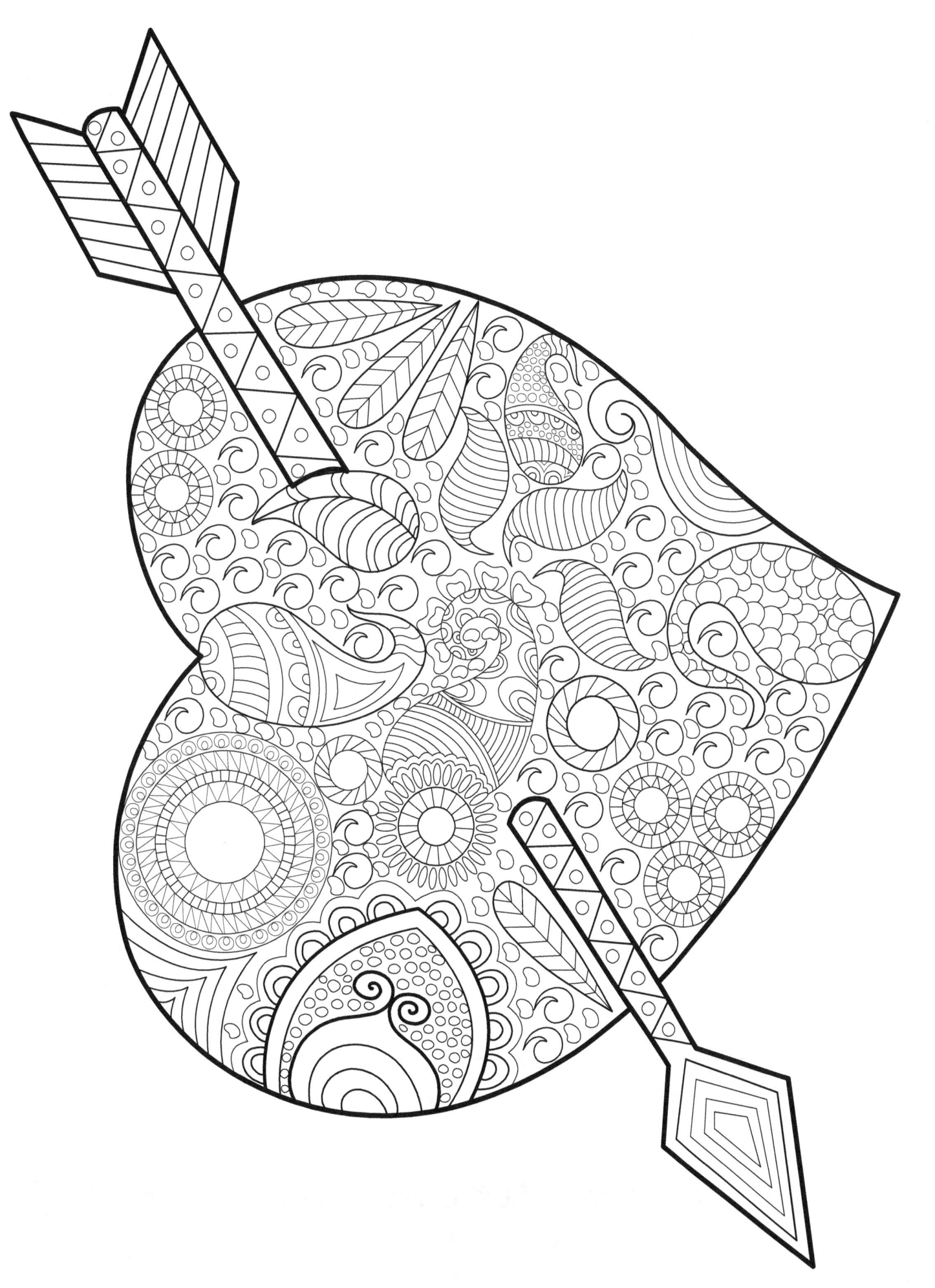

Copyright © Queen Press

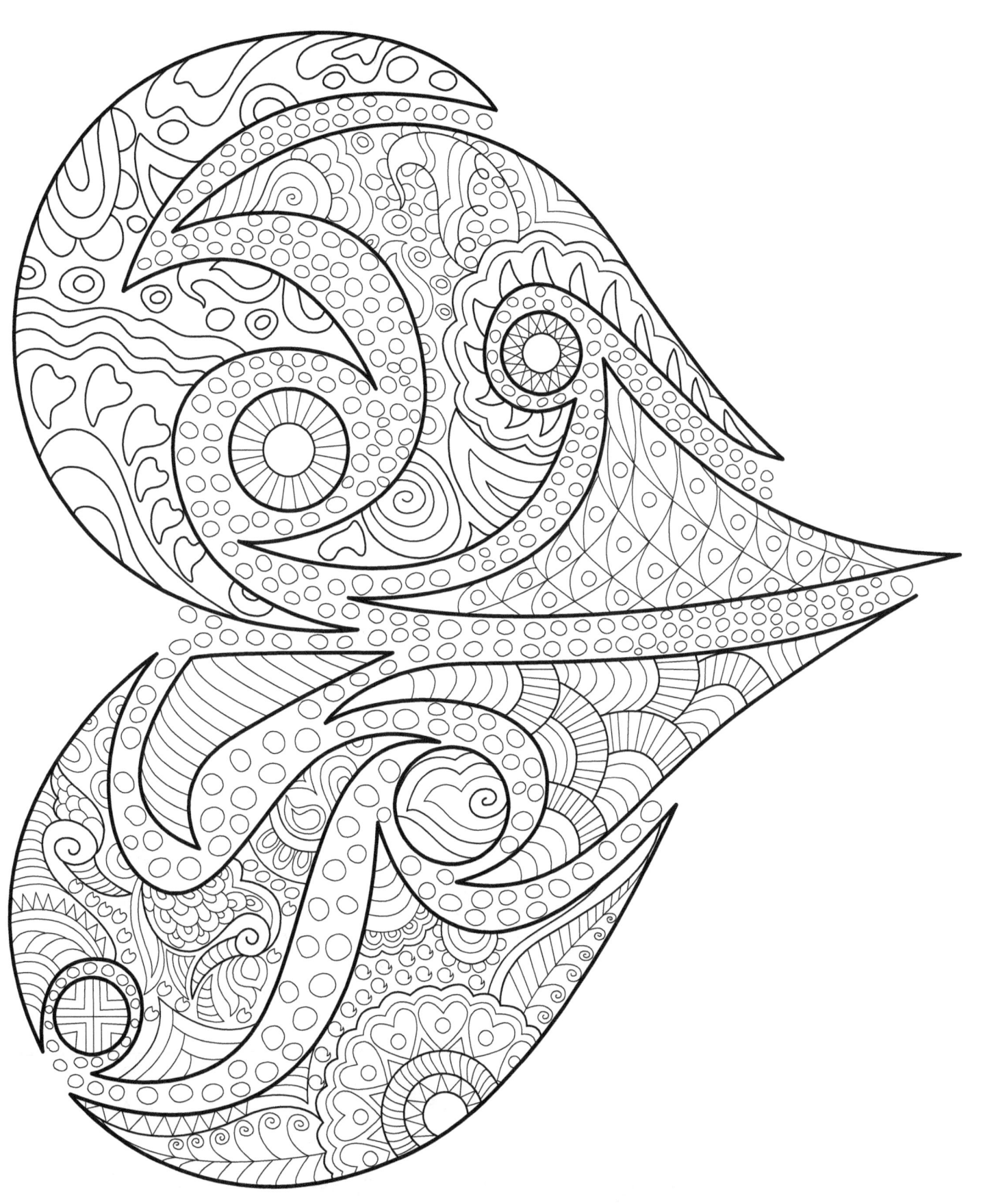

Copyright © Queen Press

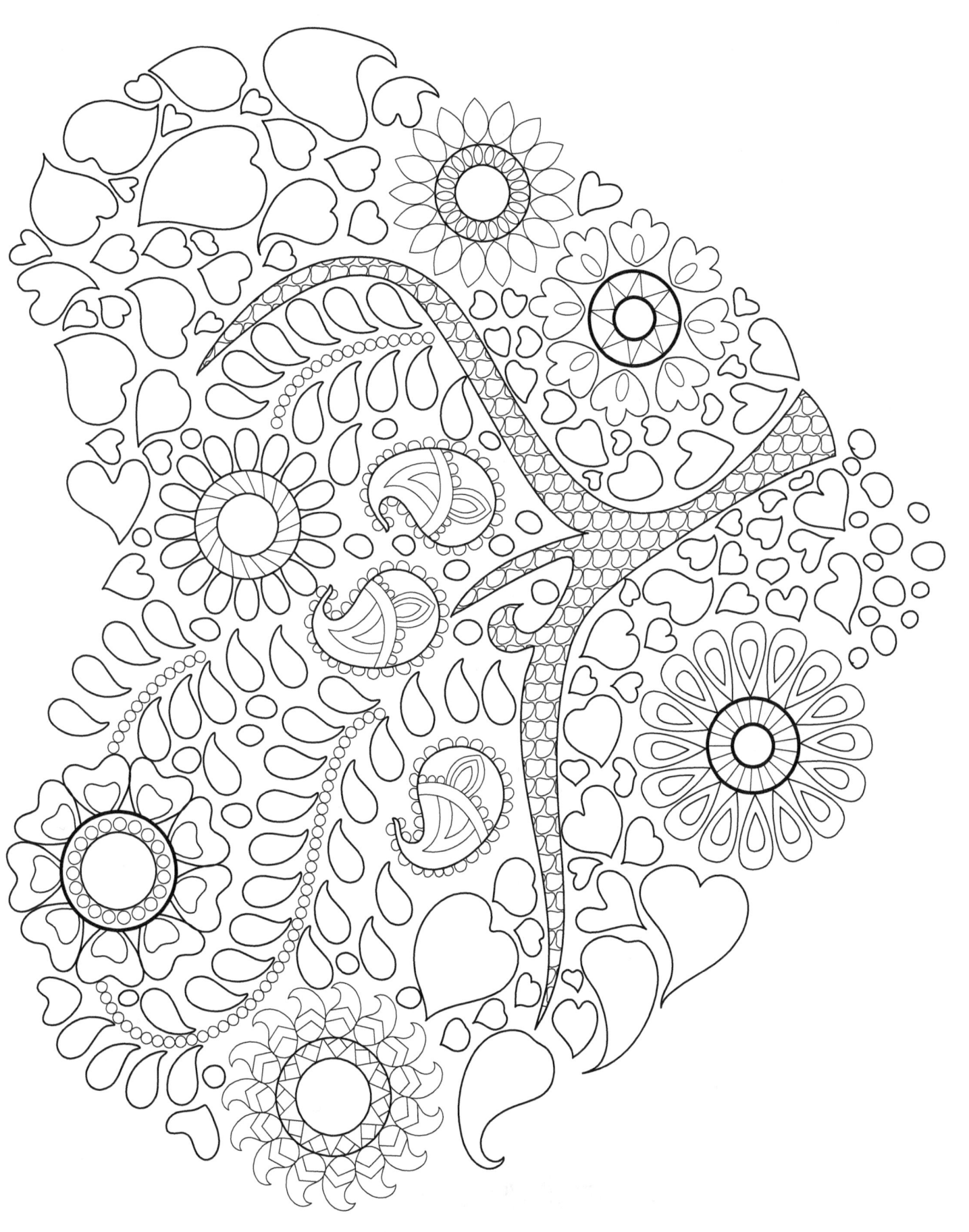

Copyright © Queen Press

www.ingramcontent.com/pod-product-compliance
Lightning Source LLC
Chambersburg PA
CBHW080623220526
45466CB00010B/3439